THE ROYAL FAMILY

First published in April 2020

A catalogue record for this book is available from the British Library.

ISBN 978 1 78521 665 7

Library of Congress control no. 2019945935

Interior styling and page design: Adelle Mahoney
Cover design: Mecob Design Ltd
With thanks to PA Images for supplying the majority of photographs.
All images are credited within the captions.

Published by Haynes Publishing,
Sparkford, Yeovil, Somerset, BA22 7JJ, UK.
Tel: 01963 440635
Int. tel: +44 1963 440635
Website: www.haynes.com

Haynes North America Inc.,
859 Lawrence Drive, Newbury Park,
California 91320, USA.

Printed in Malaysia.

THE ROYAL FAMILY

CONTENTS

THE BRITISH
MONARCHY IN
CONTEXT

WHAT IS MONARCHY?

Strictly speaking, a monarchy is a state ruled by one single, absolute ruler with supreme authority. However, over time, the role of a monarch has evolved, particularly with the wider enfranchisement of the people and the spread of democracy. In the United Kingdom and in the Commonwealth realms such as Australia, New Zealand and Canada, a constitutional monarchy and Parliamentary democracy system of government is in place. Under this system, the monarch is the head of state but reigns and does not govern or rule in accordance with the constitution. This means that Queen Elizabeth II effectively no longer has a political or executive role, but nevertheless plays an important part in the life of the nation.

The Queen Elizabeth II reigns not by the 'Grace of God' as her full titles say, but by the will of Parliament and the Act of Settlement of 1701. If it so chooses, Parliament can get rid of her and pick a successor. Furthermore, although we have a 'hereditary' monarchy, it is tradition, not law, that says that the monarch will be followed by his or her eldest son (or daughter, now the rules on primogeniture have been changed to not give preference to a male heir). Parliament is the supreme authority of the nation and has for more than 700 years gradually reduced the powers of the monarch to effectively nothing. Essentially, a monarch's role is to 'be' not to 'do'.

Primogeniture

Primogeniture is the law or custom that entitles the firstborn legitimate son to inherit his parent's entire or main estate, rather than having to share it with all or some of his siblings, or an illegitimate child or more distant relative, which was the system adopted by the royal family until 2013. The Succession to the Crown Act 2013, however, repealed the Royal Marriages Act 1772, thus replacing male-preference primogeniture with absolute primogeniture for those born in the line of succession after 28 October 2011. This means that the eldest child, regardless of sex, precedes his or her brothers and sisters. In current succession it means that Prince William and the Duchess of Cambridge's second child, Princess Charlotte, is ahead of her younger brother, Prince Louis, in the line of succession.

Monarchy in the modern world

Monarchy used to be the main form of national government around the world. By 1914, at the outbreak of World War I, only three European countries were republics – France, Portugal and Switzerland. Today, most European countries are republics. European countries that retain constitutional monarchies include Britain, Norway, Sweden, Belgium, the Netherlands and Spain. Across the world, 45 sovereign nations have monarchs acting as heads of state, 16 of which are Commonwealth realms that recognise the Queen as their head of state and where she retains a legal and ceremonial role but has limited or no political power.

ELECTED MONARCHS

Sometimes a monarch is elected, such as in the case of the Pope of the Roman Catholic Church, who rules as sovereign of the Vatican City State, but is elected for life by the College of Cardinals. In other places, such as Malaysia, the federal king is elected for a five-year term from among and by the hereditary rulers of nine of the federation's constitutive states. The United Arab Emirates also has a procedure for electing its monarch.

The English monarchy and the Church

Successive English (and later British) monarchs since King Henry VIII have all been known by the title Defender of the Faith – in Latin, Fidei Defensor (males) or Fidei Defensatrix (females). Ironically, in light of the break with Rome that the king subsequently instigated, the title

THE GREAT SEAL OF STATE

Used to show the monarch's approval of important state documents, the Great Seal of the Realm is a symbol of the sovereign's role as head of state. In 2001 a new Great Seal, 15cm (6in) in diameter and with a design by the sculptor James Butler, was introduced because the old metal die, in use since 1953, was wearing out.

Did you know?
A Royal Peculiar or Royal Peculier is a Church of England parish or church that is subject to the direct jurisdiction of the monarch and not to that of the diocese.

THE STRUCTURE OF THE CHURCH OF ENGLAND

The Church of England is Protestant, with a hierarchy of bishops similar to the Catholic church, but with the present Queen as supreme governor. As such, she is its titular head, but is not an ordained priest and is not responsible for its spiritual direction. The Queen appoints, on advice, its bishops, and all clergy swear allegiance to her. According to her coronation oath, she must be a communicant of the Anglican Church and must uphold its continued existence as the country's official religion. It means, too, that the monarch is formally of higher rank than the sitting Archbishop of Canterbury as primate.

Monarch
(Supreme Governor)

Archbishop of Canterbury
(Primate of All England)

Archbishop of York
(Northern Province)

Archbishop of Canterbury
(Southern Province)

Bishops
Dioceses

Suffragan Bishops
(assistants to Bishops in a specific part of the Diocese)

Deaneries
(a group of parishes in a locality)

Vicar/Rector
15,000 Parishes

Curates

---

was first bestowed on Henry VIII by Pope Leo X on 11 October 1521 in recognition of his treatise Defence of the Seven Sacraments (Assertio Septem Sacramentorum), which defended the sacramental nature of marriage and the supremacy of the Pope. When Henry broke with Rome nine years later, in 1530, and was established as head of his new Church of England, the title was revoked by Pope Leo's successor, Pope Paul III, and the king was immediately excommunicated.

However, in 1544, the English Parliament conferred the same title, Defender of the Faith, on the king and all his successors. This time, the title was given not for defending Catholicism but for Henry's role and position in the new Anglican faith, of which he and subsequent regents remained supreme governors, with the exception of Henry's Roman Catholic daughter Mary I.

This tradition continues to this day. When Elizabeth II was crowned Queen Regnant at Westminster Abbey in 1953, she was styled 'Elizabeth II of the United Kingdom of Great Britain and Northern Ireland and Her other Realms and Territories Queen, Head of the Commonwealth, Defender of the Faith'. Fidei Defensor is represented on all British coins by the abbreviation, 'F D' or 'FID DEF'.

The Queen, Prince Charles, Prince Harry and the Duchess of Sussex, and Prince William and Duchess of Cambridge with Princess Charlotte, Savannah Phillips and Prince George, on the balcony of Buckingham Palace, following the Trooping the Colour ceremony at Horse Guards Parade as the Queen celebrates her official birthday, June 2018. (PA Images)

ENGLISH AND BRITISH ROYAL DYNASTIES

The Normans (1066–1154)

Members of this dynasty were originally Vikings who settled in north-west France in the 10th century and later became Dukes of Normandy.

👑 In 1066, William the Conqueror – William I (1066–87), who had a claim to the English throne – defeated Saxon King Harold at the Battle of Hastings. Thereafter, a new regime was imposed on the country, with William confiscating Anglo-Saxon estates and handing them to his Norman supporters.

👑 William was succeeded by his third son, William II (1087–1100), who crushed a rebellion against Norman rule as well as pushing back two invasions by the Scots.

👑 He was succeeded by his brother, Henry I (1100–35), a reformer who expanded the system of travelling justices in the shires, in order to maintain order.

👑 On the king's death, his grandson Stephen (1135–1154) usurped the throne from Henry's only daughter, Matilda – an action that led to a civil war. Order was only restored when Henry of Anjou, the father of the House of Plantagenet and Matilda's son, made the

barons recognise him as the rightful heir to the throne and he was crowned Henry II in 1154.

House of Plantagenet (1154–1399)

This 331-year period was dominated by three major conflicts at home and abroad. It was a time that also saw Parliament evolve into a power in its own right, along with judicial reforms. The bubonic plague or 'Black Death' undermined military campaigns and ravaged the population.

The dynasty name is said to have derived from a nickname adopted by Geoffrey, Count of Anjou – the father of the first Plantagenet king, Henry II – and refers to his habit of wearing a sprig of broom or planta genista in his helmet.

👑 Henry II (1154–89) is regarded the greatest of the 13 monarchs of this dynasty, being blessed with intelligence and physical prowess.

👑 His son Richard I (1189–99) – 'Richard Lionheart' – was an archetypal medieval warrior king. Noble, fierce and courageous, he also loved poetry, music and fine clothing – attributes that helped him to capture the imagination of the people of his age.

👑 Richard was succeeded by his brother King John (1199–1216). A maverick of the dynasty, John was feckless and unstable and his reign was dominated by armed disputes with the barons, who rose in rebellion against his rule. He was forced into compliance and at Runnymede, near Windsor, on 15 June 1215, he signed the historic Magna Carta or the Great Charter, a document that curtailed royal power in matters of taxation, justice, religion and foreign policy.

COMMON Q&As

Q) What is a royal family?
A) *The immediate family of a reigning monarch, plus, sometimes, the extended family, including cousins. It can also occasionally refer to the extended relations of a deposed monarch.*

Q) What is a royal house?
A) *A royal house does not refer to where a member of the royal family lives. Instead, it is a dynastic term, whereby a royal dynasty is sometimes referred to as 'the House of xxx' (followed by the chosen name).*

Q) What is line of succession to the throne?
A) *The British line of succession is the list of people who will be the next king or queen. It excludes Catholics and illegitimate children. Traditionally, it was based on a system of primogeniture of the male heir, which meant that the oldest son became king, even if he had an older sister. Only if there were no male could a princess become queen.*

Q) What is a regent?
A) *From the Latin* regens, *'[one] ruling', a regent is a person who is appointed to administer the state because the monarch is a minor (under the age of 18), or is absent or incapacitated. The title 'Prince Regent' is given officially to a prince who acts as regent.*

Next came John's son, Henry III (1216–72), who inherited a kingdom in a state of anarchy at the age of just nine. A grandson of Henry II and Eleanor of Aquitaine, he was also the great-great-grandson of Louis VI of France. A cultivated and kind-natured man, he was seen as rather ineffectual and perhaps the most obsessive patron of art and architecture ever to have occupied the throne of England.

His son Edward I (1272–1307), by contrast, was interested in conquest and tried to build a British empire with England taking the lead. He conquered Wales, making his eldest son Edward the first Prince of Wales, and then went on to try to conquer Scotland. This failed, and Scotland retained its independence until late in the reign of the Stuart kings.

Despite this, it was his son Edward II (1307–27) who was said to have been Edward I's only failure. Openly homosexual, Edward II was devoted to his male favourites and was ultimately forced to abdicate the throne to his 14-year-old son, Edward III.

Edward III (1327–77) was one of the most charismatic and prominent personalities of his age, whose reign was dominated by the Hundred Years War (1137–1453) between England and France.

At the end of the Plantagenet period, the reign of Richard II (1377–99) – the 'Black Prince' eldest son of the valiant Edward III – saw the beginning of the Wars of the Roses, with the Crown disputed and fought over by two family strands, the Lancastrians and the Yorkists.

House of Lancaster (1399–1461)

This was a short dynasty of three kings, all called Henry and coming from a branch of the Plantagenet family. A turbulent time, the period was dominated by war and internal baronial rebellion.

The first monarch, Henry IV (1399–1413), was born at Bolingbroke Castle in 1366 and was the son of John of Gaunt and Blanche Plantagenet, daughter and heiress of Henry of Grosmont, 1st Duke of Lancaster.

He was succeeded by his son, Henry V (1413–22), who revived his great-grandfather Edward III's claim to the French throne and led an English army into France in 1415, thereby renewing the Hundred Years War. He famously won the Battle of Agincourt in 1415, defeating the French against all odds in an action that was seen as a spectacular triumph.

A few years later, upon his death, Henry V was succeeded by his infant son Henry VI (1422–61). This Henry grew to be a devout and gentle man but later displayed signs of mental illness. This resulted in his

This portrait of Richard III is the earliest surviving painting of the king, thought to be copied from a prototype that was created during his reign (1483–85). (PA Images)

cousin Richard, Duke of York, being appointed lord protector during this period, which led to conflict with Queen Margaret of Anjou and a fight for the Crown in which the Duke of York was killed.

His son retaliated and defeated the Lancastrians, and was crowned king at Westminster in 1461, becoming Edward IV. However, Edward IV was forced to flee the country and the Earl of Warwick – the so-called 'kingmaker' – restored Henry VI to the throne. Henry VI met his death, probably at the hands of Edward IV and his brothers, in the Tower of London in May 1471.

House of York (1399–1461)

This is another branch of the Plantagenet family that produced three kings: Edward IV; his son the boy king Edward V (1483); and his uncle Richard III. All three descended from the male line of Edmund of Langley, 1st Duke of York and the fourth son of Edward III.

Edward IV (1461–70 and 1471–83), was an able ruler who, restored by the justice system and the royal finances, reigned in relative peace.

His son Edward V (1483), one of the infamous 'Princes in the Tower', was declared illegitimate in 1483 and presumed murdered with his younger brother after being deposed by his uncle Richard III.

Richard III (1483–85), king for barely two years, has been much maligned throughout history and in popular culture, where he has been dismissed as a hunchback tyrant. He lost the Crown to Henry Tudor when he was killed after coming a sword's length from Tudor in the thick of the Battle of Bosworth Field in 1485.

House of Tudor (1485–1603)

This dynasty with its five regents (six if you include 'the nine day Queen', Lady Jane Grey in 1553) is among the most well known and notorious in royal history, and for good reason. The Tudor period lasted for 118 years, during which England became one of the world's most powerful countries both in terms of might and influence. For instance, the habits of the Tudor court were at the forefront of the cultural Renaissance of Europe, giving rise to some of the most famous names in literature, from Shakespeare and Marlowe to Spenser and More. The Tudor era also witnessed the most sweeping religious changes in England since the arrival of Christianity, which affected every aspect of national life. The Reformation eventually transformed an entirely Catholic nation into a predominantly Protestant one.

Of Welsh origin, Henry VII (1485–1509) succeeded in ending the Wars of the Roses between the houses of Lancaster and York and acceded to the throne after beating Richard III at the Battle of Bosworth.

👑 Henry's second son, Henry VIII (1509–47), was an autocrat who was feared and famed for the dissolution of the monasteries, the break with Roman Catholicism and having six wives. He had three children, all by different queens: Edward VI (1547–53), Mary I (1553–58) and Elizabeth I (1558–1603).

👑 Edward VI (1547–53) was Henry VIII's only legitimate son. He came to the throne as a minor, so his uncle Edward Seymour, 1st Duke of Somerset, ran the country as lord protector until he was overthrown by the Earl of Warwick in 1549. In 1553, Edward VI, aged 15, was struck by tuberculosis that eventually killed him. During his short reign, the English Reformation was consolidated.

👑 Lady Jane Grey (1553) was a cousin of the Edward and the great-granddaughter of Henry VII. She was just 15 when devious politicians made her queen. She 'reigned' for just nine days in 1553 before being overthrown by Edward's elder sister, Roman Catholic Mary. Lady Jane was later executed.

👑 Mary I (1553–58) was a devout Roman Catholic, like her mother Queen Catherine of Aragon. She was dubbed 'Bloody Mary' for her ruthless persecution of Protestants in her unsuccessful bid to restore Roman Catholicism to England. Her marriage to Philip II of Spain was childless so on her death the throne passed to her sister Elizabeth.

👑 Elizabeth I (1558–1603), the last and possibly the greatest of the Tudor monarchs, reigned during the great Elizabethan Age, during which England emerged as a major European power. Dubbed 'The Virgin Queen', Elizabeth's politically inspired decision not to wed, and consequent lack of an heir, resulted in the end of the Tudor dynasty. James VI of Scotland, son of her cousin Mary Queen of Scots, was crowned James I of England upon her death.

This portrait of the family of Henry VIII, artist unknown, is on display at Hampton Court and is basically a dynastic propaganda device. An enthroned Henry, centre, is flanked by his son, Edward, and Jane Seymour (posthumous), his third wife and mother to Edward. His two daughters, Mary, left and Elizabeth, right, are separated by pillars from the core family group of three. (Getty).

Did you know?

After extensive scientific tests, a skeleton discovered underneath a car park in Leicester in 2012 was confirmed as being that of Richard III, with a twisted spine. On 26 March 2015, Archbishop of Canterbury Justin Welby presided over a service to mark the reburial of Richard in Leicester Cathedral.

House of Stuart (1603–1714)

This Scottish House included the first monarchs of what became the United Kingdom. The ensuing Stuart dynasty witnessed the Great Plague, the Great Fire of London and lengthy and bloody wars. It was an age of intense religious debate and radical politics, both of which contributed to a bloody civil war in the mid-17th century between Crown and Parliament.

👑 When King James VI of Scotland became also King James I of England (1603–25), the two thrones were combined for the first time and the union of the kingdoms was formed.

👑 His son, Charles I (1625–49), however, faced grave discord as the Cavaliers and the Roundheads waged a bitter civil war, resulting in a Parliamentary victory for Oliver Cromwell and the eventual execution of Charles I.

👑 The era that followed is known as the Interregnum: the period between the execution of Charles I on 30 January 1649 and the arrival of his son Charles II (1660–85) in London on 29 May 1660 – the moment that marked the start of the Restoration of the monarchy. During the Interregnum, England was under various forms of republican government.

👑 Charles II was succeeded by his brother James II (1685–88), a devout Catholic whose religion and policies led to a clash with both Church and Parliament that meant he was forced to abdicate and flee to live abroad in exile.

👑 William III, William of Orange, and Mary II, James II's daughter, then reigned as joint monarchs (1689–1702) as defenders of Protestantism.

👑 They were followed by Queen Anne (1702–14), the second of James II's daughters. During her reign, Britain re-established itself as a major European power. The prospect of the end of the Stuart line, with the death of Queen Anne's only surviving child in 1700, led to the drawing up of the Act of Settlement in 1701, which stipulated that only Protestants could hold the throne.

House of Hanover (1714–1901)

The start of the Hanoverian period saw conflict and discontent, because the coronation of the first king, George I – the nearest Protestant in the line of succession according to the Act of Settlement – inspired the Jacobite rebellions led by the usurped Catholic Stuart heirs who felt they were the legitimate monarchs and had a greater right to the throne. The latter stages of the Hanoverian period, however, were much more

settled, seeing such advances as the Great Reform Act being passed in 1832, which among other things widened the electorate. It was also in this period that Britain came to acquire much of its overseas empire, despite the loss of the American colonies. By the end of the Hanoverian period, the British Empire covered one-third of the globe.

👑 In 1714, the Crown of England was passed by the 1701 Act of Settlement to Queen Anne's German Protestant cousin George I (1714–27) – a man who was, astonishingly, 52nd in line to the throne at that time. The Act effectively excluded the hereditary Stuart heir, James II's Catholic son, James Francis Edward Stuart, who was referred to as the 'Old Pretender'.

👑 George I was succeeded by his son, George II (1727–60) – the last British monarch not to be born in the country. Lacking in self-confidence, George II

Charles II in his coronation robes as the Stuart monarchy was restored to the throne after 11 years of the Interregnum, the only Republican period of Britain's history. (Getty)

relied heavily on his ministers. Despite this, he had a passion for all things military and fought the French at the 1743 Battle of Dettingen, which was the last time a British king appeared on the battlefield.

👑 George III (1760–1820) came next, the grandson of George II, and served for 60 years – a record at the time. He became unfairly dubbed 'the mad king who lost America' because he was on the throne during the American Revolutionary War, after which the colonies gained independence. He also suffered from the disorder porphyria, which rendered him unfit to rule in the last decade of his long reign. As a result, his eldest son acted as Prince Regent from 1811 until his father's death in 1820.

👑 As George IV (1820–30), the Prince Regent became king, although the title did not in reality add to the powers that he had possessed as Prince Regent. Extravagant and louche, he was a great patron of the arts and architecture, backing the work of architect John Nash, who developed Regent Street and Regent's Park, restored Windsor Castle and patronised Nash's Royal Pavilion at Brighton.

👑 William IV (1830–37) succeeded his brother George IV because the king's only direct heir, his daughter Princess Charlotte died in childbirth (along with her stillborn son), at the age of 21, in 1817. Known as the 'Sailor King', William joined the Royal Navy aged just 13 and was a friend of Lord Horatio Nelson. As king, he

King George III in coronation robes. This third Hanoverian monarch was the first in his line to be born and brought up in England. (PD)

opposed Parliamentary reform but eventually signed the 1832 Reform Bill, which lessened the power of the Crown and landowning aristocrats.

👑 Queen Victoria (1837–1901) succeeded her uncle at the age of 18. The granddaughter of George III, she died aged 81 after reigning for 63 years, seven months and two days, surpassing her grandfather's record in terms of both age and length of reign. The Victorian period was politically stable and saw the development of constitutional monarchy as Parliament gained more power from the Crown, as well as a great expansion of the British Empire. She had nine children with husband, her first cousin, Prince Albert Saxe-Coburg-Gotha, whom she married in 1840, having met him when she was just 17.

House of Saxe, Coburg and Gotha (1901–17)

This royal house was short-lived. It was created on the death of Queen Victoria in 1901, when the royal house took the Germanic surname of her consort, Prince Albert of Saxe-Coburg-Gotha.

👑 Victoria's eldest son, Edward VII (1901–10), was to become the only sovereign to complete his reign under this dynasty's banner. Members of the House of Saxe-Coburg-Gotha occupied the thrones of other European countries, including Belgium, Portugal and Bulgaria.

House of Windsor (1917–present)

The current royal dynasty of the House of Windsor was created at the height of World War I, when George V changed the family name from Saxe-Coburg-Gotha to the more English-sounding name of Windsor. This proved a wise move as one of the most important roles of the Windsor monarchs was to act as national figureheads during the devastating wars of 1914–18 and 1939–45.

👑 Edward VII's second son, George V (1910–36), had brothers-in-law and cousins with German titles such as Duke and Duchess of Teck and Prince and Princess of Battenberg. Near the start of George's reign, with World War I raging, anti-German feeling was at its peak. Some of this was directed at the royal family, for example when acclaimed writer H.G. Wells wrote about Britain's 'alien and uninspiring court'. A furious George is said to have responded, 'I may be uninspiring, but I'll be damned if I'm alien.' As a result, on 17 July 1917 the king decided to appease British nationalist feelings by issuing a royal proclamation that changed the name of the British royal house to Windsor, thus rendering himself the first Windsor monarch.

George reigned during a time of great change, not least rapid modernisation and the development of mass-communication technologies. George V was quick to see the advantages of radio to broadcast across the British Empire, and made numerous radio broadcasts that were transmitted internationally. Advances in transport also meant that members of the Windsor dynasty could travel more easily around the Empire than at any earlier time. As Prince of Wales, Edward VIII successfully carried out scores of overseas and domestic visits, making him and the royal family very popular.

👑 The story of Edward VIII (January–December 1936) and Mrs Wallis Simpson, who had been divorced once and was married to another man when she and Edward met, is well known, and led to one of the biggest crises in modern royal history, eventually costing Edward the Crown. Concern about Edward's private life had been growing in the Cabinet, opposition parties and the Dominions during the affair, and Edward realised that he had to choose between the Crown and Mrs Simpson who, as a divorcee, was not acceptable as Queen Consort. On 10 December 1936, Edward VIII therefore executed an Instrument of Abdication, which was given legal effect the following day. In essence, it meant that Edward VIII and any children he might have were excluded

George VI, father of Queen Elizabeth II, on the day of his coronation, 12 May 1937. (PD)

from succession to the throne. Instead of remaining king, therefore, in 1937 Edward was created Duke of Windsor and married Wallis Simpson. He lived abroad until the end of his life, dying in 1972 in Paris. He is buried beside Frogmore Mausoleum at Windsor. He was never crowned; his reign lasted only 325 days.

👑 Edward's younger brother, the Prince Albert, Duke of York, became king and was crowned in May 1937, taking the name George VI (1936–52). George VI was dutiful and determined, although hampered by a stutter, and adapted to the role with the support of his wife, the former Lady Elizabeth Bowes Lyon, later Queen Elizabeth. His greatest achievements came as a leader during World War II. Throughout the conflict the king, who developed a close working relationship with Winston Churchill, remained at Buckingham Palace, despite it being bombed nine times. He regularly broadcast to the nation and visited severely bombed areas. He died following a lung operation, on 6 February 1952 at Sandringham, aged 56.

👑 George VI was succeeded by his eldest daughter, Queen Elizabeth II (1952–present), the current monarch and the focus of much of this book.

Did you know?

The Duchess of Windsor, who was never awarded the title Her Royal Highness, is buried beside Edward VIII in Frogmore royal burial ground beside Queen Victoria's mausoleum in Windsor Great Park.

RUSSIAN INFLUENCE

Queen Victoria was baptised Alexandrina, after her godfather Alexander I of Russia. She preferred to go by her second name, Victoria, or the nickname 'Drina'. At birth, she was fifth in the line of succession for the British Crown, behind the four eldest sons of George III, including her three uncles and her father, Edward, Duke of Kent.

HER MAJESTY THE QUEEN, ELIZABETH II

FACTS

BIRTH DATE: *21 April 1926*

BIRTH PLACE: *Mayfair, London*

TITLES (UK): *Her Majesty Elizabeth the Second, by the Grace of God, of Great Britain, Ireland and the British Dominions beyond the Seas Queen, Defender of the Faith*

OCCUPATION: *Head of state*

MARRIED DATE: *20 November 1947*

FAN OF: *Singers Petula Clark, Matt Monro and Sammy Davis Jr. She also likes the occasional Dubonnet cocktail before lunch, made of fortified wine added to a glass of gin with sliced lemon*

AVERSION TO: *Beatle John Lennon, whom she regarded as 'vulgar' after the two met following the Royal Variety Performance in 1963. The Queen was said to be delighted when he sent back his MBE in 1969*

Queen Elizabeth II (1952–present) has been on the throne for longer than any other monarch in British history. In that time, she has travelled more widely than any other king or queen and has undertaken many historic overseas visits. As such, she has been an important figurehead for Great Britain and the Commonwealth, the voluntary association of 53 independent countries, almost all formerly under British rule, of which she is head.

When she was born at 17 Bruton Street, Mayfair, the then Princess Elizabeth did not expect that she would one day become monarch. However, when her uncle King Edward VIII abdicated on 10 December 1936, Edward agreed that he and any children he might have would be excluded from the succession of the throne and that his younger brother, Elizabeth's father Prince Albert, Duke of York, become King George VI. This meant that the princess was his direct heir, known as heir presumptive and, unless George and the Queen Consort had a male heir, that Elizabeth would be the next monarch.

On 6 February 1952, King George VI died and Princess Elizabeth acceded to the throne, becoming Her Majesty Queen Elizabeth II (although some Scots state that she

is Elizabeth I of Scotland because Henry VIII's daughter Elizabeth I was only Queen of England, not Scotland.) The following year, on 2 June 1953, the coronation took place. The event, the first televised coronation, meant millions around the Commonwealth could share every moment.

Head of state

As head of state, the monarch undertakes constitutional and representational duties that have evolved over 1,000 years of history. The monarch is formally head of state as well as head of the nation and has a special relationship with the prime minister of the day, with whom he or she has a private weekly audience. As head of state, the monarch has only three rights: to be 'consulted' by the prime minister; to 'encourage' certain courses of action; and to 'warn' against others. The monarch's less formal role of 'head of nation' means that he or she acts as a focus for national identity, unity and pride and thus helps to provide a sense of continuity in the country.

Commander-in-chief

As sovereign, Queen Elizabeth II is head of the Armed Forces and holds many military appointments and honorary ranks. She is also the wife, mother and grandmother of individuals who have served in the Forces, and was the first female member of the royal family to join the Armed Services – the Auxiliary Territorial Service (ATS) in 1945 – as a full-time active member.

All of this means that the Queen has long had close links with the Armed Forces, both in the UK and in the Commonwealth, and over the course of her reign, she has made regular visits to service establishments and ships. During these trips she meets many servicemen

Did you know?

The Queen's birthplace, 17 Bruton Street in Mayfair, is now a Cantonese restaurant called Hakkasan. Although the house, formerly the London home of her maternal grandparents, no longer exists, a plaque to record the birth of the Queen was placed on the site in 2012.

and women of all ranks, and their families. She also meets service personnel at investitures, when she awards various military honours, including the Elizabeth Cross. Instituted in 2009, this was the first medal to which the Queen put her name, and is given in special recognition to the families of those who died on military operations or as a result of terrorism since 1948.

Royal engagements

The Queen has always carried out a full programme of engagements – something that she continues to do despite the retirement of her consort, Prince Philip, in May 2017, with her full support. Duties range from visits to charities and schools to hosting visiting heads of state, and leading the nation in Remembrance and celebratory events. She is supported by her heir, Prince Charles, and members of the royal family, particularly when it comes to carrying out overseas travel; now in her 90s, the Queen no longer takes long-haul flights.

Royal recognition

The Queen has links as royal patron or president with more than 600 charities, military associations, professional bodies and public service organisations. She regards this as one of the most important aspects of her role as it allows the various entities' achievements and contributions to society to be recognised.

The Queen also encourages achievement by presenting honours to the general public at investitures and by hosting palace garden parties, receptions and other awards given in her name for those who have contributed to the nation and the Commonwealth.

The line of succession

While anything is possible, the line of succession will not change should Prince Charles predecease his mother the Queen. In that situation, Prince William will take his father's place as heir apparent and become King of Great Britain when the Queen dies, or Prince Regent if she decides to step down from her role as monarch.

The Queen at the opening of one of the UK's biggest veterans' housing projects in October 2019, at Haig Housing Trust's estate in Morden. This is London's largest community of ex-service personnel, which has been in place now for over 100 years. (G. Edmondson/Jobson Media)

In a toned down ceremony in terms of pomp and regalia, Queen Elizabeth sits on the Sovereign's Throne, with Prince Charles beside her, to deliver the Queen's Speech at the State Opening of Parliament on 14 October 2019. (PA Images)

ROYAL JUBILEES

The Queen's reign has been punctuated by a series of milestones. She has now celebrated her Silver, Golden, Diamond and Sapphire jubilees and her birthdays have provided cause for national celebration, often in the form of street parties and other community events. On 9 September 2015 the Queen became Britain's longest-reigning monarch.

Monarch and the heir to the throne

The reigning monarch is not obliged to share sensitive state information with her direct heir and in the past this has caused conflict between the two incumbents, notably Queen Victoria and her heir, the future King Edward VII, when he was Prince of Wales. The current Queen and Prince of Wales, however, meet regularly, in private, and in the interests of continuity he, as her direct heir, has access to government papers. Prince Charles also conducts regular meetings with ministers of the Crown and visiting heads of state and foreign dignitaries.

Although the heir to the throne has no formal job description as such, the main part of his role is to support the monarch as the focal point for national pride, unity and allegiance. As a figurehead, he brings people together across society, representing continuity, highlighting achievement and emphasising the importance of service.

These two people, reigning monarch and the heir to the throne, whether male or female, are the two most important when it comes to the line of succession to the British throne.

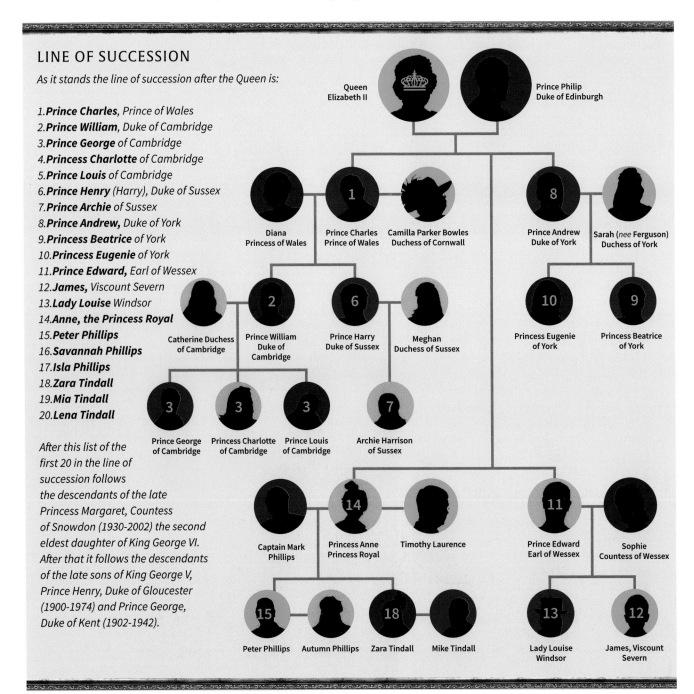

LINE OF SUCCESSION

As it stands the line of succession after the Queen is:

1. **Prince Charles**, Prince of Wales
2. **Prince William**, Duke of Cambridge
3. **Prince George** of Cambridge
4. **Princess Charlotte** of Cambridge
5. **Prince Louis** of Cambridge
6. **Prince Henry** (Harry), Duke of Sussex
7. **Prince Archie** of Sussex
8. **Prince Andrew**, Duke of York
9. **Princess Beatrice** of York
10. **Princess Eugenie** of York
11. **Prince Edward**, Earl of Wessex
12. **James**, Viscount Severn
13. **Lady Louise** Windsor
14. **Anne, the Princess Royal**
15. **Peter Phillips**
16. **Savannah Phillips**
17. **Isla Phillips**
18. **Zara Tindall**
19. **Mia Tindall**
20. **Lena Tindall**

After this list of the first 20 in the line of succession follows the descendants of the late Princess Margaret, Countess of Snowdon (1930-2002) the second eldest daughter of King George VI. After that it follows the descendants of the late sons of King George V, Prince Henry, Duke of Gloucester (1900-1974) and Prince George, Duke of Kent (1902-1942).

Queen Elizabeth II — Prince Philip Duke of Edinburgh

Diana Princess of Wales — Prince Charles Prince of Wales — Camilla Parker Bowles Duchess of Cornwall

Prince Andrew Duke of York — Sarah (nee Ferguson) Duchess of York

Catherine Duchess of Cambridge — Prince William Duke of Cambridge

Prince Harry Duke of Sussex — Meghan Duchess of Sussex

Princess Eugenie of York

Princess Beatrice of York

Prince George of Cambridge

Princess Charlotte of Cambridge

Prince Louis of Cambridge

Archie Harrison of Sussex

Captain Mark Phillips — Princess Anne Princess Royal — Timothy Laurence

Prince Edward Earl of Wessex — Sophie Countess of Wessex

Peter Phillips — Autumn Phillips

Zara Tindall — Mike Tindall

Lady Louise Windsor

James, Viscount Severn

HRH PRINCE CHARLES

Prince Carles is the eldest son of Queen Elizabeth II and Prince Philip, Duke of Edinburgh. The safe arrival of Charles Philip Arthur George was announced just before midnight on the evening of the birth, and led to celebrations around the country and Commonwealth.

In the hereditary monarchal system, the heir to the throne is often, but not always, given the title His Royal Highness the Prince of Wales. Just 21 men have held the rank. History has shown that the majority of those were great supporters of and servants to their sovereign and the Crown. In a few cases, however, the heirs have been more trouble than they were worth. Among the unscrupulous few are those who secretly plotted to overthrow the reigning monarch in a bloody power grab, while others displayed unfitting behaviour that seriously undermined the sitting monarch.

Charles' investiture as Prince of Wales by the Queen took place on 1 July 1969 in a ceremony at Caernarfon Castle. Before the elaborate ceremony, the Prince, who studied at Trinity College at Cambridge University, where he was awarded a 2:2 in History, spent a term at the University College of Wales at Aberystwyth, learning to speak Welsh. Following his formal education he joined the Royal Navy and served on the guided missile destroyer HMS Norfolk and two frigates. He also qualified as a helicopter pilot in 1974 before joining 845 Naval Air Squadron, which operated from the Commando carrier HMS Hermes. On 9 February 1976,

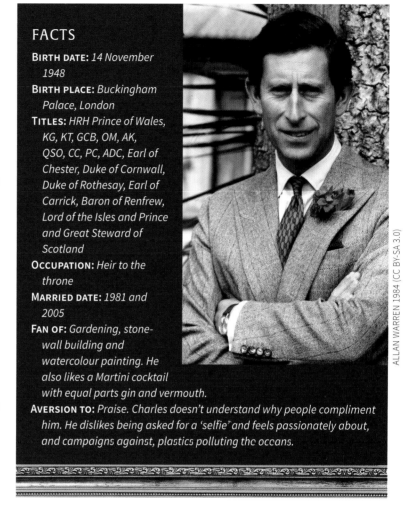

FACTS

BIRTH DATE: *14 November 1948*

BIRTH PLACE: *Buckingham Palace, London*

TITLES: *HRH Prince of Wales, KG, KT, GCB, OM, AK, QSO, CC, PC, ADC, Earl of Chester, Duke of Cornwall, Duke of Rothesay, Earl of Carrick, Baron of Renfrew, Lord of the Isles and Prince and Great Steward of Scotland*

OCCUPATION: *Heir to the throne*

MARRIED DATE: *1981 and 2005*

FAN OF: *Gardening, stone-wall building and watercolour painting. He also likes a Martini cocktail with equal parts gin and vermouth.*

AVERSION TO: *Praise. Charles doesn't understand why people compliment him. He dislikes being asked for a 'selfie' and feels passionately about, and campaigns against, plastics polluting the oceans.*

ALLAN WARREN 1984 (CC BY-SA 3.0)

Far left: Prince Charles acts as guide for his mother, during his time as a Royal Navy sub-lieutenant aboard HMS Norfolk. June 1972. (PA Images)

Left: Charles is handed his flying helmet by a ground crewman before going up for his first 'dual control' flight with instructor Lt Commander Alan MacGregor in a Royal Navy Wessex V helicopter, September 1974. (PA Images)

PRINCES OF WALES

The title Prince of Wales represents the continuity of English and Welsh and, latterly, British, history. The bearer has no formal public role or responsibility legislated by Parliament but is usually the next in line to the throne, or heir apparent. The title Earl of Chester has always been bestowed upon the recipient in conjunction with it. The title Prince of Wales is not automatically given, and the title can not be inherited, either. It can be a poisoned chalice, too – and has in the past been a role immersed in intrigue, peril and even murder.

What links all the bearers is that each of them was heir to the throne of England or Great Britain. There is, however, little affiliation other than that. Ten of the 21 were created Prince of Wales as adults or youths and eight as children. Only a select few have held the title for more than a decade, with a two princes holding it for barely a year. Nor has the title guaranteed the holder reached the throne.

the prince took command of the coastal mine-hunter HMS *Bronington* for his last nine months of service.

Marriages

The prince has been married twice. First to Diana, Princess of Wales (29 July 1981 at St Paul's Cathedral, London), the mother of his two sons, Prince William and Prince Henry (Harry) of Wales. The couple divorced in 1996, and Diana was killed in a car accident in Paris a year later along with her lover Dodi Fayed, and the driver of the car Henri Paul. Charles married his second wife, Camilla Parker Bowles (born 17 July 1947), on 9 April 2005 in a civil ceremony at the Guildhall, Windsor, followed by a Service of Prayer and Dedication at St George's Chapel, Windsor.

ALL IN A NAME

Technically, Camilla, Duchess of Cornwall is also HRH the Princess of Wales. However, she chose not to use the title in order to avoid causing offence to those who still admire Diana, Princess of Wales. The next person to take the title will be Catherine, the Duchess of Cambridge, when William is named the Prince of Wales. Camilla will also become Queen Consort when Charles becomes King, although Clarence House did say it was her intention to instead take the title Princess Consort if the moment came.

The Prince's Trust

As heir to the throne, Prince Charles has devoted his life to public duty, supporting the Queen in her role as head of state, as well as being a global philanthropist. The Prince's Trust, which he founded in 1976 to help vulnerable young people get their lives on track, has helped more than 870,000 young people turn their lives around. It has also created more than 125,000 entrepreneurs since its creation.

Campaigning prince

Prince Charles has been widely lauded for his work as a pioneer and campaigner on climate change and environmental issues. He is acknowledged by some as a powerhouse behind a global sustainability revolution, urging world leaders to think more deeply about how we are treating nature and the planet and to realise – for the sake of future generations – that lifestyles must change. 'Right action cannot happen without right thinking' is one of his key messages on the issue.

Throughout his life, the prince has striven to make a real difference and to enlighten others. He has championed organic farming and spoken up for sustainable urbanism, emphasising the need for local character to be preserved. He has encouraged a more balanced approach to business and healthcare and a more benign and holistic approach to science and technology.

Charles's stance on some big issues has placed him in the firing line for daring to challenge the current orthodoxy and the conventional way of thinking, but

what the prince has actually been revealing is that all of these areas are interrelated. He argues that we must all see what he often calls 'the big picture' – to appreciate the problems humanity faces.

Changing times, changing royals

In 1953, when the Queen ascended the throne on the death of her father, times were very different, with a society that was more generally Anglican-led Christian. For instance, many believed that Elizabeth II had been appointed by God. Prince Charles, however, will become head of a very different, multi-denominational nation, and by the time his son William succeeds him, according to census analysis, Christianity could no longer be the prevailing faith.

Treading lightly in a more diverse society can be difficult, and Charles has faced some criticism from detractors who claim that his apparent lack of faith and his alleged less-than-solid relationship with the established church, the Church of England, means that he is not fit to be king. It is true that Charles displays a

Diana, now Princess of Wales, and Prince Charles on the steps of Westminster Abbey after their wedding service, 29 July 1981. (PA Images)

Did you know?

Prince Charles rarely eats lunch. He does enjoy a cup of tea, however. His favourite is Darjeeling with honey and milk. The Queen, meanwhile, has a supply of tea specially blended for her by Twinings.

CHARLES AND RELIGION

As Christians and as members of the Church of England, both Charles and Camilla regularly attend church. When in Scotland, they attend the Church of Scotland and, when travelling abroad, Anglican churches. They also regularly meet Church leaders and attend engagements with the Christian community from many Christian denominations. In a bid to enact Christian principles, he has spent his working life trying to encourage dialogue and good relations between Britain's main faith communities.

willingness to embrace and work alongside other faiths and has long been an advocate of the importance of interfaith dialogue, but it does not logically follow that his bid to build bridges automatically demonstrates a lack of commitment to being a Christian and to the Church of England. Despite claims to the contrary, Charles will be named as 'Defender of the Faith' when he is crowned king.

Could Charles become Prince Regent?

Some close to the Queen say that if she reaches the age of 95, she may make a monumental decision and choose to officially allow her heir, Prince Charles, to take over the stewardship of her reign. This would entail the Queen officially transferring all executive powers to Charles as Prince Regent until her death, when he will become king. This would enable her to fudge the issue of not fulfilling her coronation oath, whereby she swore to God and her people to serve as queen regnant until her death.

Abdication does not have the same negative connotations as it did when the Queen's uncle renounced the throne. In 2014 King Juan Carlos of Spain abdicated in favour of his son, Felipe, after 39 years on the throne, and even the Catholic Church survived a papal abdication. For some reason, though, some commentators insist that Elizabeth should stay in position no matter what her age. Can we seriously expect her to remain as head of state if she lives to be a centenarian like her mother?

Unlike in Spain, where politicians had to amend the constitution to accommodate Juan Carlos's decision, in the UK we already have the Regency Act enshrined in law. The last time such provisions were used was in 1810 during the reign of George III, when the monarch became permanently deranged and his eldest son assumed the title Prince Regent for 10 years until, on his father's death, he became George IV.

Queen Elizabeth II, by contrast, has enjoyed remarkably good health, both mental and physical, and there is nothing to suggest that a regency would be necessary in the way that it was for George III. Prince Charles has always been consistent about his position: his ascension is 'in the lap of the gods', he has said.

Prince Charles is officially welcomed to the Caribbean 'Spice Island' Realm of Grenada. He is being greeted by Dame Cecile La Grenade (also pictured), the country's Governor General, after the RAF State Voyager jet landed in the capital St George's. (Jobson Media)

Did you know?
The first formal photograph of Prince Charles was taken by the famous Cecil Beaton in December 1948.

HRH PRINCE WILLIAM

William is the second in line to the throne and the elder son of the Prince of Wales and Diana, Princess of Wales. He married Catherine Middleton (born 9 January 1982), whom he met at St Andrew's University when they were both undergraduates, at Westminster Abbey on 29 April 2011. William and Catherine, now titled the Duchess of Cambridge, have three children: Prince George, Princess Charlotte and Prince Louis. Their official residence is Kensington Palace. William undertakes a number of charitable activities and projects and carries out public and official duties in support of the Queen, in the UK and overseas. Having completed seven-and-a-half years of full-time military service, promoting the welfare of those who are serving or who have served their country in the Armed Forces is a key focus for his charitable work. Other key areas are conservation and supporting communities to protect the natural world, young people, and mental health, which he supports along with his wife through the Royal Foundation of the Duke and Duchess of Cambridge.

FACTS

BIRTH DATE: *21 June 1981*
PLACE OF BIRTH: *St Mary's Hospital, London*
TITLES: *The Duke of Cambridge, The Earl of Strathearn and Baron of Carrickfergus, KG, KT, PC, and ADC to the Queen.*
OCCUPATION: *Heir to the heir of the throne*
MARRIED DATE: *29 April 2011*
FAN OF: *Aston Villa Football Club*
AVERSION TO: *Public displays of emotion, and any hint of a 'royal soap opera' developing*

HRH Prince George of Cambridge (born 22 July 2013)

George is the first child of the Duke and Duchess of Cambridge and therefore is third in line to the throne. He was born in St Mary's Hospital in Paddington, London, on 22 July 2013 and weighed 8lb 6oz (3.9kg). He was christened George Alexander Louis on 23 October 2013 at the Chapel Royal, St James's Palace by the Archbishop of Canterbury, Justin Welby. In keeping with royal tradition, Prince George wore a hand-made replica made by Angela Kelly, dressmaker to the Queen, of the original Victorian royal christening robe. The Lily Font and water from the River Jordan were also used during the baptism. In April 2014, Prince George accompanied his parents on their official three-week tour of New Zealand and Australia, and received a warm welcome in both countries. Along with his sister, Princess Charlotte, he later accompanied his parents on their official visit to Canada, and in July 2017 again joined his parents, with his sister, on an official tour to Poland and Germany.

FUN FACTS ABOUT WILLIAM

- *Prince William was born on Midsummer's Eve, making him a solstice baby. According to astrological experts: 'Those born during the magical cusp of the summer solstice quickly fall under the spell of enchantment. Romantic and inspirational, they often put their talents and energies in service of a higher purpose.'*
- *Prince William got his name after 'a bit of an argument', according to sources. Princess Diana chose William while Charles's choice, Arthur, went second, followed by Philip in honour of Charles's father, and Louis for the heir to the throne's much loved great-uncle, Louis Mountbatten, who was assassinated in 1979.*
- *An accident in 1991 left the Prince with what he calls his 'Harry Potter' scar, still visible today, which he obtained when a schoolfriend accidentally hit him on the forehead with a golf club.*
- *When Prince William joined the RAF in 2008 he was known by his fellow airmen as 'Billy the Fish' – a pun on the name 'William Wales'.*
- *Prince William is a keen surfing fan and he has enjoyed riding the waves in St Andrews, Cornwall and Devon as well as Portugal.*

Prince William and Catherine with Princess Charlotte and Prince George on an official royal tour of Poland at Chopin Airport in Warsaw July 2017. (PA Images)

HRH Princess Charlotte of Cambridge (born 2 May 2015)

Charlotte is the second child of the Duke and Duchess of Cambridge and is fourth in line to the throne. She is the first royal child to be impacted by the change in the law of primogeniture, meaning that by virtue of being older, she is higher up the line of succession than her younger brother Prince Louis of Cambridge. She was born in St Mary's Hospital, London on 2 May 2010, and weighed 8lb 3oz (3.75kg). Named Charlotte Elizabeth Diana, the princess was baptised at the Church of St Mary Magdalene, Sandringham on Sunday 5 July 2015.

Members of the local community were invited to join in the occasion outside the church.

HRH Prince Louis of Cambridge (born 23 April 2018)

Louis Arthur Charles is the third child of the Duke and Duchess of Cambridge and is behind his sister Princess Charlotte in the line of succession. Prince Louis was born at 11.01am on 23 April 2018 at St Mary's Hospital in Paddington, London, weighing 8lb 7oz (3.95kg). He was christened at the Chapel Royal at St James's Palace in London on 9 July 2018.

Princess Charlotte arrives for her first day of school, with her brother Prince George and her parents the Duke and Duchess of Cambridge, at Thomas's Battersea in London 5 September 2019. (PA Images)

THE REST OF THE ROYALS IN ORDER OF SUCCESSION

Prince Henry, Duke of Sussex (born 15 September 1984)

Popularly known as Prince Harry, Henry is sixth in line to the throne and the younger son of the Prince of Wales and Diana, Princess of Wales. Harry married American actress Rachel Meghan Markle (born 4 August 1981) at St George's Chapel, Windsor on 19 May 2018 and as his wife she took the title of Duchess of Sussex.

A career soldier, Prince Harry spent a decade in the Armed Forces, ending operational duties in 2015. During this period, he conducted two tours of duty to Afghanistan with the British Army. Harry is passionate about promoting the welfare of those serving their country in the Armed Forces. His Invictus Games – an international adaptive sporting event for both serving and veteran wounded, injured and sick service personnel – set up in 2014 – has been a major success.

In January 2020 Harry and Meghan announced on Instagram that they had decided to step back from their role as senior royals, '... after many months of reflection and internal discussions'. They said they planned to balance their time between the UK and North America, initially on the island of Vancouver in British Columbia, Canada, while, 'continuing to honour our duty to the Queen, the Commonwealth, and our patronages'. The Queen responded by saying she regretted their decision, but was 'entirely supportive' of it. It was agreed that Prince Harry and Meghan would no longer use their HRH titles, although they would retain them, that the couple would receive no public funds or formally represent the Queen while carrying out royal duties. Together with his wife, Harry now directs his philanthropic work through their own foundation.

ARCHIE HARRISON MOUNTBATTEN-WINDSOR (BORN 6 MAY 2019)

Archie is the first child of the Duke and Duchess of Sussex and is behind his father Prince Harry in the line of succession, at seventh. He was born in a private hospital at 5.36am on 6 May 2019 weighing 7lb 3oz (3.25kg) and is the first member of the royal family with Afro-American heritage; his mother, US-born Meghan, Duchess of Sussex, is of dual heritage. Archie was baptised in the private chapel at Windsor Castle on 6 July 2019 by the Archbishop of Canterbury, Justin Welby. Members of the St George's Chapel Choir performed at the ceremony. The Duke and Duchess of Sussex kept the service, and the identities of the godparents, private.

Prince Harry and Meghan introduce their son, Archie Harrison Mountbatten-Windsor, to Archbishop Tutu in Cape Town during their official tour of South Africa in October 2019. (Jobson Media)

HARRY AND MEGHAN

Prince Harry's joint royal monogram with his wife Meghan features their individual monograms intertwined into one elegant design with a small crown at the top. The crown features two crosses pattée – a type of Christian cross – four fleurs-de-lis, and two strawberry leaves.

Did you know?

As part of the Walking With The Wounded South Pole Allied Challenge of 2013, Prince Harry became the first and only member of the Royal Family to reach the South Pole.

Prince Andrew and the Duchess of York, with their daughters Beatrice (L) and Eugenie, arriving for the European Premiere of 102 Dalmations at the Odeon cinema, in Leicester Square, London, December 2000. (PA Images)

HRH Prince Andrew, Duke of York (born 19 February 1960)

The Duke of York is the third child and second son of Queen Elizabeth II and Prince Philip, Duke of Edinburgh. He is eighth in line to the throne. In 1979 Andrew joined the Royal Navy and had a 22-year active service career. After leaving the Royal Navy, the Duke became the UK's Special Representative for International Trade and Investment working with the government, and UK Trade and Investment (UKTI). On his marriage to Sarah Ferguson (born 15 October 1959), he was created the Duke of York. The couple were divorced in 1996. They have two daughters, Princesses Beatrice and Eugenie, who follow Andrew in the line of succession.

In November 2019 Buckingham Palace announced that the Duke of York was stepping back from all royal duties, 'for the foreseeable future'. Andrew stepped down after facing persistent questions over his links to US financier and convicted sex offender, Jeffrey Epstein, who committed suicide while awaiting trial on sex-trafficking charges in August 2019.

Prince Edward, and Sophie, Countess of Wessex, with their children, Lady Louise and James, Viscount Severn feeding a giraffe during a visit to the Wild Place Project in Bristol in July 2019. (PA Images)

HRH Prince Edward, Earl of Wessex (born 10 March 1964)

Prince Edward is the fourth and youngest child of the Queen and the Duke of Edinburgh. He married Sophie Rhys-Jones, now the Countess of Wessex (born 20 January 1965), at St George's Chapel, Windsor, in 1999. He is a full-time working member of the royal family and together with his wife supports the Queen in her official duties, as well as undertaking public engagements for a large number of his own charities.

Edward has assumed many duties from his father, since he retired from public life in 2017, had has succeeded him as president of the Commonwealth Games Federation, after being vice-patron since 2006, and opening the 1990 Commonwealth Games in New Zealand and the 1998 Commonwealth Games in Malaysia. He has also taken over his father's role in the Duke of Edinburgh's Award Scheme. His son James,

HRH Princess Anne with Sportswoman of the Year award, December 1971, awarded to the person who has done most to enhance British sporting prestige internationally. (PA Images)

Viscount Severn (born 17 December 2007) and daughter Lady Louise Windsor (born 8 November 2003), follow him in the line of succession.

HRH Princess Anne, Princess Royal (born 15 August 1950)

Princess Anne, the Princess Royal, is the second child and only daughter of the Queen and the Duke of Edinburgh. Known for a dutiful work ethic and her charitable work as patron of over 200 organisations, she is viewed by some as one of the most popular and respected members of the royal family. She is a renowned equestrian talent, having won one gold medal (1971) and two silver medals (1975) at the European Eventing Championships, and was the first member of the British royal family to have competed in the Olympic Games. She was awarded the title of Princess Royal by the Queen in 1987, and is the seventh holder of the title.

Princess Anne has been married twice. First to Captain Mark Phillips in 1973; they divorced in 1992. They have two children and four grandchildren. In 1992, within months of her divorce, Anne married Vice Admiral Sir Timothy Laurence, whom she had met while he served as her mother's equerry between 1986 and 1989.

Anne is followed in the line of succession by her son Peter Phillips (born 15 November 1977) and his children

with wife Autumn Kelly (married 2008): Savannah Phillips (born 29 December 2010) and Isla Phillips (29 March 2012). They are followed in the line of succession by Princess Anne's daughter Zara Phillips (now Tindall) MBE (born 15 May 1981), a world champion eventing rider and Olympian in the Great Britain Eventing Team. She married rugby union England international player Mike Tindall on 20 July 2011 in Scotland. Their children Mia Tindall (born 17 January 2014) and Lena Tindall (18 June 2018) follow her in the line of succession.

From left: Prince Charles, Prince Harry, Prince William, Peter Phillips (eldest son of Princess Anne), Sophie the Countess of Wessex, and Prince Edward – all share a joke as they watch a parade in the Mall as part of the Queen's Golden Jubilee celebrations, June 2002. (PA Images)

ROYAL MILITARY RECORDS

Above: Princess Elizabeth receives vehicle maintenance instruction on an Austin 10 Light Utility Vehicle while serving with No 1 MTTC at Camberley, Surrey with the Auxiliary Territorial Service (ATS). (PA Images)

Above right: The Duke of Edinburgh – wearing the uniform of Admiral of the Fleet – speaks at a lunch in Guildhall, London. (PA Images)

The royal family has long had a close link with the military, and the Queen remains head of the Armed Forces. In addition, many current royals have played an active part in the Services or combat situations.

Prince Philip

Prince Philip had joined the Royal Navy as a cadet in 1939 and after successfully completing his training spent six months in the Indian Ocean as midshipman aboard the battleship HMS *Ramillies* in 1940. In 1941, while serving on the HMS *Valiant*, Philip was mentioned in despatches for his actions in the Battle of Matapan after spotting an unexpected enemy vessel with the searchlights. He was later awarded the Greek War Cross of Valour. He was then promoted to sub-lieutenant and served on destroyer HMS *Wallace*. In 1944, Philip was appointed first lieutenant and second-in-command of the new fleet destroyer HMS *Whelp*, which sailed to the Indian Ocean to join the British Pacific Fleet. In 1952, Philip was promoted to commander, but was forced to cut short his naval career when his wife became queen.

Prince Charles

On 8 March 1971 Charles started jet pilot training at Royal Air Force (RAF) Cranwell in Lincolnshire. After passing out with his wings in September, the prince started his Royal Navy career. A few years later, in 1974, he also qualified as a helicopter pilot and went on to join 845 Naval Air Squadron, which operated from the Commando carrier HMS *Hermes*. On 9 February 1976,

Charles took command of the coastal mine hunter HMS *Bronington*, where he remained for the last nine months of his time in the Royal Navy.

Prince Charles holds the highest honorary rank in all three of the Armed Forces: Field Marshal, Admiral of the Fleet and Marshal of the Air Force.

Prince Andrew

Prince Andrew joined the Royal Navy on a short-service commission as a seaman officer, sub-specialising as a pilot. The following year he began fixed-wing and helicopter flight training at RAF Leeming and then Royal Naval Air Station Culdrose. Having achieved the rank of sub lieutenant, Prince Andrew next converted to pilot of the Sea King helicopter, before joining his first front-line unit: 820 Naval Air Squadron (NAS) embarked

ATS QUEEN

Princess Elizabeth insisted on joining the Auxiliary Territorial Service (ATS) in 1945, aged 18. She started as a subaltern and in so doing the future queen became the first female royal to join the Armed Services as a full-time member. By the end of the World War II Princess Elizabeth had reached the rank of junior commander, having successfully completed her course at No.1 Mechanical Training Centre of the ATS, and she also passed out as a fully qualified driver.

in HMS *Invincible* – part of the task group that sailed to the South Atlantic to regain the Falkland Islands in April 1982. During the conflict Andrew took part in many types of mission, including anti-submarine warfare, anti-surface warfare, inter-ship helicopter delivery, and search and rescue.

Andrew went on to remain in active service with the Royal Navy for a total of 22 years, Towards the end of his military career, in 1997, Andrew was appointed to the Ministry of Defence as a staff officer in the Directorate of Naval Operations. He left active service in July 2001.

Edward, Duke of Kent

The Queen's first cousin, the Duke of Kent served in the Armed Forces in the UK and overseas for 22 years, from 1955–76. In 1993, he was promoted to field marshal. The Duke retains close links to the Army and visits his regiments regularly, including when they were engaged in combat operations in Iraq and Afghanistan. As royal colonel and a personal aide-de-camp to the Queen he has represented the Queen at memorial services.

Prince William

Having graduated from St Andrew's university, Prince William joined the Royal Military Academy Sandhurst as an officer cadet. After completing his 44-week training course, he was commissioned as an Army officer in December 2006 and joined the Household Cavalry (Blues and Royals) as a second lieutenant. A year later, he was promoted to the rank of lieutenant.

William next decided to pursue a flying career in the military and began training as a search and rescue pilot in early 2009. Following various skill-based training exercises and exams, Flight Lieutenant Wales, as he was known in the RAF, joined C Flight, 22 Squadron at RAF Valley in Anglesey in September 2010 as a search and rescue pilot. During his three years in this role, William undertook 156 search and rescue operations, undertook a routine operational deployment to the Falklands, and qualified as an operational captain. His honorary ranks are: Major, British Army; Lieutenant Commander, Royal Navy; Squadron Leader, Royal Air Force.

Prince Harry

Harry began his military career as an officer cadet at the Royal Military Academy Sandhurst in May 2005 and was later commissioned as a second lieutenant in the Household Cavalry (Blues and Royals). He then served with the British Armed Forces for a decade, during which time he undertook two operational tours of Afghanistan, the first between 2007 and 2008 as a forward air controller. Shortly after returning to the UK Harry was promoted to the rank of lieutenant with the Household Cavalry and began training as an Army Air Corps pilot in 2009. Following completion of the course, he trained as an Apache attack helicopter pilot and became fully operational in February 2012. At the end of that year, he undertook his second tour of duty to Afghanistan and in July 2013 he qualified as Apache aircraft commander.

In early 2014, Harry completed his attachment to the Army Air Corps and transferred to a staff officer role in HQ London District. At this time he helped to organise the inaugural Invictus Games in London. In March 2015, it was announced that after a fulfilling military career, Harry would leave the Armed Forces. During his final weeks, he was seconded to the Australian Defence Force. As he left operational service in June 2015, he said: 'The experiences I have had over the last 10 years will stay with me for the rest of my life. For that I will always be hugely grateful.' Until Spring 2020, Harry's honorary ranks were: Lieutenant Commander, Royal Navy; Squadron Leader, Royal Air Force.

Prince William, the Duke of Kent and Princess Anne during Trooping of the Colour ceremony on the Mall and at Buckingham Palace, June 2012. (Shutterstock)

Below left: Prince Charles attends a Navy College passing out parade at HMS Collingwood, April 2003. (Shutterstock)

THE
COMMONWEALTH
AND THE CROWN

FROM EMPIRE TO COMMONWEALTH

The concept of the Commonwealth was established in the 19th century when the British Empire was at its zenith and its flag flew over every continent. By the time the Empire covered 21 million sq km (13 million sq miles) and contained 458 million people, however, nations were demanding greater independence and the British Empire had begun to be disassembled, with many countries seeking to become dominions. The Empire was thus changing, such that in 1884 politician Lord Rosebery described it as, 'a commonwealth of nations'.

The creation of the Commonwealth

In 1867 Canada became the first colony to be transformed into a self-governing 'dominion' – a newly constituted status that suggested equality with Britain. Other parts of the Empire followed suit quite soon afterwards – Australia in 1901, New Zealand in 1907, South Africa in 1910 and the Irish Free State in 1922.

After World War I, the dominions sought a new constitutional definition and in 1926 the Balfour declaration was adopted. This defined the dominions as self-governing communities within the British Empire that were to be equal in status, in no way subordinate to one another in their domestic or external affairs, and also united by common allegiance to the Crown. This definition was incorporated into British law in 1931 as the Statute of Westminster, creating the British Commonwealth of Nations. It was adopted immediately in Canada, the Irish Free State, Newfoundland (which

joined Canada in 1949) and South Africa. Australia and New Zealand followed shortly after. India, Britain's largest colony at the time, became a dominion at Independence in 1947 and remained so until January 1950, when the Indian Republic was created.

The new Commonwealth dropped the word 'British' from its name and the allegiance to the Crown from its statute in 1949, welcoming nations that had been former colonies. To reconcile the aims of the new Commonwealth, the 1949 London Declaration recognised George VI as Head of the Commonwealth. Following his death, although it is not a hereditary role, Commonwealth leaders recognised Elizabeth II in that capacity, too. We also know Prince Charles will take over from her because Commonwealth leaders announced

> ## CURRENT COMMONWEALTH REALMS
>
> 1. Antigua and Barbuda
> 2. Australia
> 3. The Bahamas
> 4. Barbados
> 5. Belize
> 6. Canada
> 7. Grenada
> 8. Jamaica
> 9. New Zealand
> 10. Papua New Guinea
> 11. St Kitts and Nevis
> 12. St Lucia
> 13. St Vincent and the Grenadines
> 14. Solomon Islands
> 15. Tuvalu
> 16. United Kingdom

The Queen and Commonwealth leaders, taken at the 1960 Commonwealth Conference, Windsor Castle. Front row: (left to right) EJ Cooray, Walter Nash, Jawaharlal Nehru, Elizabeth II, John Diefenbaker, Robert Menzies, Eric Louw Back row: Tunku Abdul Rahman, Roy Welensky, Harold Macmillan, Mohammed Ayub Khan, Kwame Nkrumah (PD)

that this would be the case at the Commonwealth Heads of Government Meeting (CHOGM) 2018 in London. The ruling does not apply to Charles's direct heir, Prince William.

The Queen's role

The Queen is sovereign of 16 Commonwealth realms including the United Kingdom. She is also Head of the Commonwealth itself, a voluntary association of 53 independent countries. She regards the Commonwealth as one of the successes of her reign, saying at the CHOGM in Malta in 2015: 'I feel enormously proud of what the Commonwealth has achieved, and all of it within my lifetime'. The Queen's role is largely symbolic and is seen as being one of unity; as the association's head, the Queen reinforces the links by which the Commonwealth joins people from around the world.

MAINTAINING CLOSE CONTACT WITH THE COMMONWEALTH

Although the Queen no longer makes overseas visits, she keeps in touch with Commonwealth developments through close contact with respective prime ministers, as well as through the London-based Commonwealth Secretary General, and her Secretariat. She also has regular meetings and conversations with heads of government from Commonwealth countries. In addition, the Queen attends the Commonwealth Day celebrations in London, including an inter-denominational service held in Westminster Abbey.

Above: Prince Charles after laying a wreath during a commemorative service at the Commonwealth War Graves Commission's Bayeux War Cemetery in Normandy, France, 6 June 2019. (PD)

Above left: Carrara Stadium, at the Gold Coast 2018 Commonwealth Games. Hosted by Australia, this was the first major multi-sport event to achieve gender equality by having an equal number of events for male and female athletes. (PD CC BY 2.0)

COMMONWEALTH GAMES

The Commonwealth Games have been held every four years since their inception in 1930, apart from during World War II. The event has changed through the years, much like the Commonwealth of Nations it represents. Initially it was called the British Empire Games, then from 1954 to 1966 it was the British Empire and Commonwealth Games. In 1970 and 1974 it was the British Commonwealth Games, and from 1978 it became known by its present name. In addition to the 54 members of the Commonwealth, 17 overseas territories, island states and crown dependencies take part in the games.

The games symbolise the coming together of a highly diverse group of nations in a central setting as fellow human beings. Its values are echoed in the Athlete's Oath, which is taken on behalf of all the competitors at the opening ceremony of the Games, presided over by a member of the royal family: 'We declare that we will take part in the Commonwealth Games of (insert year) in the spirit of true sportsmanship, recognising the rules which govern them and desirous of participating in them for the honour of our Commonwealth and for the glory of sport.'

STATE VISITS AND TOURS

The Queen riding an elephant in a procession on a visit to India, February 1961. (PA Images)

Members of the British royal family undertake official visits every year on behalf of the Foreign and Commonwealth Office in order to enhance and protect the UK's overseas interests. Before each visit, members of the Royal Household, the royal family member's Metropolitan Police personal protection officers and the communication officer assigned to them will advance the trip and carry out extensive reconnaissance, or 'recce'. On the recce, they liaise with local security forces and officials in the host country, with the help of the British Ambassador in situ and his Embassy or High Commission staff. If the visit is to a Commonwealth realm the recce still takes place but the government of the host country, where the Queen is monarch, takes the lead in the arrangements.

State visits

When the monarch makes an overseas trip, it is known as a state visit. The Queen is the most travelled reigning monarch in history: since her first trip as sovereign in 1952 to Kenya, from which she returned as queen, she has visited more than 120 different countries, in many cases multiple times. She was also the first monarch in British history to visit China (in 1986) and Russia (in 1994) on state visits.

In contrast, the Queen's grandfather, George V, disliked foreign travel and, apart from the celebrated Imperial Indian Durbar of 1911, which became known as the 'Delhi Durbar', he made only three state visits during his reign: to Paris in 1914 and to the kingdoms of Belgium and Italy in 1922–23.

Today, however, due to her age, the Queen no longer makes these foreign forays. Her last long-haul flight was to Australia in 2011 and her last state visit was to Germany in June 2015. The previous year she paid a state visit to France, travelling by Eurostar. She now restricts her journeys to short flights, 'away-days' by royal train, commercial railway or car, all within the UK.

In her stead, Prince Charles does much of the travelling abroad, usually but not always accompanied by his wife the Duchess of Cornwall. These trips are given the same status as state visits in all but name. Charles has travelled more than any other heir to the throne in history, spreading the soft power of 'brand royal'. It is, in effect, a job-share monarchy, with the heir to the throne adopting the role of a quasi monarch carrying out overseas visits on his mother's behalf.

From Empire to Commonwealth

A year after taking the throne, the young Queen was handed a mammoth diplomatic mission: to lead the transformation from Empire to Commonwealth. This was to be her longest-ever Commonwealth tour, lasting six months, and one that would cement her position as symbolic leader of much of the free world. Setting off in November 1953, she toured 13 countries, in the West Indies, Australasia, Asia and Africa, covering 70,196km (43,618 miles). Many of these countries had never before seen their ruling monarch in person.

Following that first tour, the Queen made many repeat visits to those 13 countries, along with trips to numerous other places besides.

INDIA, PAKISTAN AND BANGLADESH

When the Queen stepped off the plane in New Delhi on 21 January 1961, she began the first visit by a British monarch since the Partition of India in August 1947. She was the 'human link' between the Commonwealth and people. Hers was an unenviable job: to try to hold the union together and convince India's millions of people that this new association was worthwhile.

The Partition of India, and the deaths it caused, was still raw in the memory of the people. Many still blamed the departing British occupiers for the horrific and bloody tragedy that had occurred. As a result, some critics questioned the wisdom of the Queen's visit to India, but the monarch defied her detractors. The visit was a success. The sovereign's strength of personality and belief in the Commonwealth and its core values shone through everywhere she went. She was warmly received, with 2 million people turning out to greet her and the Duke of Edinburgh as they drove through Delhi. Hundreds of thousands also witnessed the historical

moment when she laid a wreath on the memorial of Mahatma Gandhi, leader of the Indian nationalist movement against British rule. In so doing, the Queen pulled off a diplomatic masterstroke, wooing the Indian power brokers, the press and the people with every step.

She was received with a similarly warm welcome on a flying visit to Pakistan on the same tour, when many thousands took to the streets of Karachi shouting 'God Save the Queen'. In Peshawar, close to the Afghan border, the Queen was moved by the scenes, remarking, 'It seems to me the Pakistanis and the British have a common talent for pageantry'.

In November 1983, with Pakistan out of the Commonwealth, the Queen flew to Bangladesh, which at the time was one of the organisation's poorest and most populated countries. When the Queen arrived there was no escaping the terrible plight of many Bangladeshis. At a Save the Children centre in Dhaka, for instance, she saw for herself the effect of starvation in the desperate form of a tiny two-year-old child called Jamal, who reached out and embraced her. The normally reserved monarch was clearly moved.

The Queen and Prince Philip then flew to India for that year's CHOGM. Prime Minister Indira Gandhi greeted them at New Delhi airport. There, the Queen carried out perhaps her most unusual walkabout, from a palanquin – a traditional litter chair. The warmth of the Queen's welcome was reflected at the state banquet when Mrs Gandhi spoke of the bond between Britain and India: 'We share a wealth of common values and interests,' she said. 'A devotion to democratic ideals and to the institutions which maintain them'. A year later, Mrs Gandhi was assassinated by two Sikh bodyguards. The Queen, horrified by the killing, mourned with the Indian people, stating that: 'The world and the Commonwealth have lost one of their most distinguished leaders'.

SUBSEQUENT STATE VISITS

The Queen returned to India again in 1997 to mark the 50th anniversary of India's independence, but the visit was overshadowed by her foreign secretary, Robin Cook, who had accompanied her and who was lambasted in the press for saying that the UK could mediate between India and Pakistan in the row over Kashmir. Suddenly, press headlines were about 'new British imperialism'.

The Queen carried on regardless, laying a wreath at the spot of the worst atrocity in the history of British India at Amritsar. The wreath-laying was a gesture intended to acknowledge the excesses of a shared history, and to build on this reconciliation.

It worked. The ruling Sikh party in Punjab, the Shiromani Akali Dal, were delighted that the Queen had visited the holiest of their shrines, the Golden Temple. Not for the first time, the monarch had smoothed over potential hostility.

SRI LANKA

The Queen first visited the island during her 1954 round-the-world tour, when she opened Parliament in what she described as 'an extraordinary hall open to the elements on each side'. The island at the time was still called Ceylon, becoming Sri Lanka in 1978 when it became a republic. She visited the island again in 1981.

SINGAPORE, MALAYSIA AND BRUNEI

The Queen's first tour of south-east Asia took place in 1971–2, and included state visits to Singapore and Malaysia. During the trip, the Queen, Prince Philip and

The Queen, without shoes, leaving the Golden Temple of Amritsar in the Punjab, India, where British soldiers killed nearly 400 people in 1919. (PA Images)

Did you know?
The Queen does not have a passport. This is because they are issued in her name and on her authority, thus making it unnecessary for her to hold one. Other members of the royal family do have a passport.

Princess Anne sailed aboard the Royal Yacht *Britannia* to Kuala Lumpur, and then progressed to the states of Sarawak and Sabah, where they were greeted by members of the formerly fearsome, head-hunting Murat tribe, standing guard with 1.8m (6ft)-long blow pipes.

On the same royal tour, the Queen made her first trip to the Sultanate of Brunei Darussalam, on the northern tip of the island of Borneo. A British protectorate from 1888, it later gained its independence in 1984, and joined the Commonwealth the same year. The Sultan of Brunei, Hassanal Bolkiah, is one of the world's richest men thanks to the country's oil and gas reserves.

The Queen and the Duke of Edinburgh returned to the region in 1998 for a three-day visit. The itinerary included trips to a water village, health centre, school, and fruit and vegetable market, drinking tea with around 75 eminent professional Brunei women, and visiting the Jame 'Asr Hassanil Bolkiah Mosque. After that, the Queen visited Singapore to officially close the Commonwealth Games. The next royals to visit the region were Prince William and the Duchess of Cambridge for the Queen's Diamond Jubilee year.

MALDIVES

The Queen spent four days at sea before arriving at the Maldives, a tiny collection of islands in the Indian Ocean. While they have never been a British colony, the Maldives were once under British protection but gained independence in 1965. In 1982, the Maldives were granted special membership of the Commonwealth, reserved for states with limited financial resources, before gaining full status three years later.

On the visit, the Queen surprised the archipelago's president, Mohamed Nasheed, when she revealed that during the visit, the royal yacht had rescued some fishermen who were drifting out to sea.

AFRICA

On her first overseas tours the Queen made it her mission to get to know the leaders of the African

Commonwealth nations. Her personal relationships with powerful African politicians, such as Kenneth Kaunda of Zambia, Hastings Banda of Malawi, Daniel arap Moi of Kenya and Julius Nyerere of Tanzania, were crucial for the development of the Commonwealth on the Continent. They saw her as a mother figure, and the Commonwealth as a family, as well as a protector of their Commonwealth ideals, a belief that those who succeeded them share today.

In Africa, the modern Commonwealth continues to be relevant, as is evidenced by the fact that even countries with no historical ties to imperial Britain have applied to join, and been accepted, as members of the association. The first such country to be admitted was the former Portuguese colony of Mozambique in 1995, following its first democratic elections. The most recent was the former Belgian colony of Rwanda: it was admitted as the 54th member in 2009 and is now, after years of bloody civil war, rebuilding itself with Commonwealth help.

The birth of Zimbabwe

In 1965, Rhodesia's prime minister, Ian Smith, refused to give the 95 per cent black population the vote. In response, the Queen wrote a brief and friendly letter to Mr Smith, which was made public, clarifying that he could not claim loyalty to the monarchy and the Commonwealth and at the same time defend white supremacy. She added: 'I should be glad if you would accept my good wishes and convey them to all my peoples in your country, whose welfare and happiness I have very closely at heart.'

In 1979 the CHOGM was to be held in Zambia's capital, Lusaka. At the time, nationalists were fighting the white-minority government of Rhodesia for greater voting and political power for black Africans. Some of these guerrillas were based in Zambia, where the Rhodesian government was trying to bomb them out of existence.

As a result, Mrs Thatcher announced that for security reasons the Queen could not attend the meeting. Within 24 hours, Buckingham Palace had issued a statement stating that the Queen had every intention of going. She had never been to Zambia and felt its president needed her support. Not long before the Queen was due to arrive, a bomb exploded near President Kenneth Kaunda's offices. The Queen didn't change her plans and was greeted by a huge crowd in Lusaka. During the summit, she played an important role in the agreement to hold Rhodesian elections and a new constitution.

Kenya

Kenya has always been significant in the story of the Commonwealth and the royal family. It was, after all, the country in which Princess Elizabeth learned that she had become Queen on the death of her father. Since that historic trip, the Queen Prince Philip have visited Kenya four more times, and other members of her family have also regularly visited for holidays. It is also the place where Prince William proposed to Catherine Middleton. The couple had secretly flown into the country in October 2010 to stay in a Rutundu cabin on secluded Lewa Wildlife Conservancy. Carrying his late mother's engagement ring in his rucksack for weeks, the

Queen Elizabeth II with President Daniel arap Moi of Kenya during the ceremonial drive from Nairobi Airport, Kenya, November 1983. (PA Images)

prince finally found the perfect spot in which to propose, surrounded by beautiful lakes and wildlife.

GHANA

The close bond between Ghana and Britain was made clear in 1959 when the Queen was given a warm reception wherever she went on that visit. At the 1964 Commonwealth Conference, the then president Kwame Nkrumah also proposed the establishment of a permanent Commonwealth secretariat in order, as Nkrumah put it, 'to make the Commonwealth move in tune with the common aspirations of its members'.

The Queen last visited newly independent Ghana in 1999. In a speech during that trip she said that Ghana had been at the forefront of 'the renaissance in Africa of democratic values'.

THE QUEEN AND NELSON MANDELA

The Queen met Nelson Mandela for the first time when he was representing the African National Congress (ANC) as an observer of the Commonwealth Conference in Harare, Zimbabwe, in 1991. Nelson Mandela, who had recently been freed from prison, appeared at the Commonwealth summit ahead of the traditional banquet for government heads. The Queen broke precedent and invited him to join them at the banquet, even though he wasn't a head of government.

South Africa's first non-racial elections were held on April 1994, resulting in the election of Nelson Mandela as president. One of Nelson Mandela's first acts as president was to return South Africa to the Commonwealth of Nations. In 1961, during the apartheid era, the country had left the organisation

The Queen talks with Archbishop Desmond Tutu as she and President Nelson Mandela leave St George's Cathedral in Cape Town, after attending a service to mark human rights day, March 1995. (PA Images)

when it was decided that racial equality was a condition of membership.

The friendship between Mr Mandela and the Queen after 1994 was an enduring one. He famously referred to the Queen as 'my friend Elizabeth'. She returned the compliment and, in correspondence between the two, she signed off, 'your sincere friend, Elizabeth'. He also gave her a hand-painted silk scarf to mark South Africa's return to the Commonwealth after the apartheid years.

The two would meet many times – including during his state visit to the UK in 1996, when he stayed at Buckingham Palace.

UGANDA

The Queen and Prince Philip visited Uganda during the first Commonwealth tour in April 1954. They returned 53 years later with Prince Charles and the Duchess of Cornwall to attend the CHOGM in Kampala. On the visit, the Queen was photographed shaking hands with an HIV patient – Steven Wakodo, who was being treated at an AIDS clinic set up by the UK-based charity Mildmay – in public for the first time.

NIGERIA

In 2003, the Queen arrived in Abuja, two days ahead of the Commonwealth summit, on her first visit since the country's independence in 1960. During the intervening years Nigeria had suffered civil war, military dictatorship and corrupt rule and was suspended from the Commonwealth between 1995 and 1999. Commonwealth leaders agreed to Nigeria's reinstatement when the country embarked on its return to democracy, culminating in presidential elections to end 15 years of military rule. During the Queen's 2003 visit, she spoke of the importance of securing a free democracy, saying: 'Democracy gives people a choice in how they are governed, and those in government rule with the consent of their people.'

AUSTRALASIA

After the success of the Queen's first Commonwealth tour in 1954, which reached fever pitch on the Australian leg of the trip, many felt the links between Britain and its former colonies were assured. After all, in 1954 a million people had lined the streets of Sydney to witness the Queen's arrival, with another 500,000 standing on the foreshore, filling every vantage point.

However, when she returned to the country in 1963 on a less formal tour, the attitude towards the monarchy had cooled. According to critics, Britain's decision to join its European neighbours in the then European

Economic Community (EEC) had been at the expense of its old Commonwealth ties. Whatever the reason, support Down Under for the monarchy had shrunk, while there was a growing chorus for Australia and New Zealand to ditch their status as realms and become independent republics.

Nevertheless, a few years later the Queen prepared once more for a return to Australia and New Zealand in 1970. Her new team of advisers – led by her then press secretary, Sir William Heseltine, an Australian – were determined that this overseas tour would not be as disappointing as the last. They therefore came up with an idea of closer interaction between the Queen and her people, something she had advocated for years, but which had been vetoed for security concerns. The plan was simple: she would step out of the car before an appointment to meet and greet people in the crowd, many of whom had waited hours for a glimpse of her.

The first time she tried this was in Wellington in New Zealand on her 1970 trip. It caused a sensation; the public were thrilled that the Queen wanted to meet them before her engagements with the dignitaries. In fact, it was such a success that the 'walkabout' as it was dubbed in the press went on to become a standard feature of all subsequent royal tours for the royal family.

The relationship between the Queen and Australia has remained close, if somewhat contentious, and in 1999 Australians voted to retain the Queen as their head of state, with 55 per cent wanting to keep the monarchy. Many believe that at the end of the Queen's reign there will be another vote and Charles will not be installed

The Queen visits the Town Hall in Sydney with Emmet McDermott, Lord Mayor of Sydney, during her tour of Australia, May 1970. The walkabouts that she began in New Zealand during this tour became a tradition on all royal tours since. (PA Images)

The Queen, on her final overseas tour, delivers the inaugural address at the Commonwealth Heads of Government Meeting (COHGM) in Perth, Australia, on October 28, 2011. (PA Images)

as king. Recent polls suggest that most Australians would prefer a home-grown head of state, but that they disagree on how to go about choosing one.

The Queen and Prince Charles's position on constitutional matters is consistent: she is happy to serve as a constitutional monarch for as long as she is wanted, but believes that any change is a democratic matter for the people and country concerned. For example, in her keynote speech at the Sydney Convention and Exhibition Centre in 2000, shortly after the referendum, she said: 'I have always made it clear that the future of the monarchy in Australia is an issue for you, the Australian people, and you alone, to decide by democratic and constitutional means. It should not be otherwise.' However, she went on: 'In the light of the result of the referendum last November, I shall continue faithfully to serve as Queen of Australia under the constitution to the very best of my ability. That is my duty. It is also my privilege and pleasure.'

FAREWELL TRIP TO AUSTRALIA

When the Queen, by this time in her mid-80s, returned to Australia in 2011 for the CHOGM it was described by some in the media as her farewell tour.

Despite the 22-hour flight, she smiled and waved at the cheering crowd as she stepped off the specially chartered British Airways Boeing 777 on to Australian soil for her 16th visit to the country. As a nice touch, she was wearing an aqua Stewart Parvin-designed military coat and a diamond wattle brooch – a gift from the people of Australia during the Queen's first visit in 1954.

The brooch was not the only reminder of that historic first tour. Margaret Cunningham had been six when she was chosen to present the newly crowned Queen, then aged 27, with a posy of native flowers. All these years later, the two met again, this time on a sun-baked

airfield in the Australian capital city. Mrs Cunningham, now 64, presented the Queen with another bouquet and welcomed her back to the country. 'I said it was lovely to see her again after all these years', Mrs Cunningham confided. 'She looked at me with those same blue eyes from all those years ago.'

NEW ZEALAND

There has always been a close affinity between New Zealand, the Commonwealth and Britain, and the Queen is known to love her visits there, saying she has always felt a bond with the indigenous Maori inhabitants. This was manifested in January 1954, when the Queen was received by a huge crowd at Rotorua, complete with a traditional Maori welcome in which she and Prince Philip were presented with ceremonial cloaks. Her second visit, in 1961, coincided with Waitangi Day, the anniversary of the signing of the Treaty of Waitangi in 1840, in which representatives of the British Crown and 500 Maori chiefs agreed to found a nation and build a government together. Then, in 1981 the Queen was given the title, *Te kotuku rerenga tahi*, which means, 'the lone flight of the rare white heron'. At an official event later, the speaker, a Maori dignitary, made a prediction that Prince Charles would soon give the royal couple a grandchild. The Queen and Prince Philip burst out laughing. Just 18 days later, it was announced that Princess Diana was pregnant.

Not all the Maori people have been so welcoming, however. During subsequent visits, there have been a number of protests from Maori activists. During the Queen's 1986 trip, for example, a man lifted his grass skirt to expose his tattooed bottom at the royal motorcade, in an ancient warrior insult over the giving away of Maori rights to Britain. On another day, women protestors threw eggs at the motorcade. The Queen made light of it, saying at the banquet 'New Zealand has long been renowned for its dairy produce, though I should say that I myself prefer my New Zealand eggs for breakfast.'

RETAINING OLD TIES

In New Zealand it is far easier to vote out the monarchy than it is in its larger neighbour Australia. In Australia, constitutional change requires a majority in four of the country's six states, in addition to a majority nationally of all votes cast. New Zealand, however, does not have a federal system and a simple ballot vote could topple the Crown. Despite considerable talk by the Kiwi politicians for constitutional change, though, the appetite for it seems to have faded.

Fiji

The Queen abdicated as the monarch of Fiji in 1987 following two military coups. After the second, she knew the situation could no longer continue and said it was time to accept that Fiji was a republic. Elizabeth then instructed the governor general to resign, ending Fiji's status as a realm. The Commonwealth suspended Fiji that same year, but the island was readmitted 10 years later when democracy was restored, only to have its membership broken off again. Fiji was reinstated as a full member of the Commonwealth in 2014.

Canada

In 1939, the Queen's father, George VI, became the first reigning monarch to visit Canada, travelling by train across the country. When his wife Queen Elizabeth (later the Queen Mother) was asked whether she was English or Scottish when she arrived in Canada, she famously replied: 'Since we reached Quebec, I've been Canadian'.

The Queen has toured Canada 24 times and on her last visit there, in June 2010, she spoke of her deep bond with the country. 'My mother once said that this country felt like a home away from home for the Queen of Canada', she said. 'I am pleased to report that it still does and I am delighted to be back amongst you all.'

Her first trip to Canada was as Princess Elizabeth in 1951. It was her first royal visit and she was understandably nervous, particularly as she was worried about her father's ill health. Elizabeth and Prince Philip spent 33 days in the vast country, travelling a total of 16,000km (10,000 miles). 'From the moment when I first set foot on Canadian soil, the feeling of strangeness went', she said, 'for I knew myself to be not only amongst friends, but amongst fellow countrymen.'

Did you know?

The Queen has never been one for taking sides and admits that when England's cricketers are playing the West Indies, she finds it hard to know which team to support. She is, after all, queen of both.

Since then, the Queen and Prince Philip have visited every province in Canada. Her first visit as monarch was in 1957. At a state banquet, she wore a lavish green satin Norman Hartnell dress, adorned with a garland of green velvet maple leaves, Canada's national symbol. Canadians were thrilled. The gown became known as the 'maple leaf of Canada dress'.

Two years later the Queen returned and, alongside US President Eisenhower, opened the new St Lawrence Seaway in Canada, which connects the Atlantic with the Great Lakes in America. She also made her first live appearance on Canadian television. After the exhausting visit, however, she realised that it was impossible to cover Canada properly in a single tour. Since then, all royal tours have focused on particular provinces and often mark important occasions. For example, the Queen returned to Canada in 1967 to celebrate the Centennial of Confederation, cutting a towering 9m (30ft)-high birthday cake on Ottawa's Parliament Hill, and nearly a decade later she opened the Olympic Games in Montreal in 1976, in which Princess Anne competed as a member of the British equestrian team. Two years later, in 1978, the Queen officiated at the opening of the Commonwealth Games in Edmonton,

Queen Elizabeth II, State Secretary Judy LaMarsh and Prince Philip, Duke of Edinburgh, enjoy the Parliament Hill folk art concert in Ottawa, Canada, July 1967. (PA Images)

A HOME FROM HOME

The Queen and other members of the royal family are frequent visitors to the region, so much so that the Royal Yacht Britannia *was quite a common sight in the oceans and harbours of the Caribbean until 1997, when it was decommissioned after 44 years of service. By that time, this royal residence of the sea, which is now a floating museum in Scotland, had become one of the most famous ships in the world, hosting highly successful diplomatic receptions in its state apartments on board, as well as being the Queen's home from home on royal tours.*

and again in Victoria in 1994. In 1977, she returned to celebrate her Silver Jubilee and in 2002 she marked her Golden Jubilee by visiting the new territory of Nunavut.

Despite the Queen's popularity, Canada experienced significant republican unrest for many years, particularly during the 1960s. In recent years, those feelings have subsided and Canada is now seen as one of the most steadfast of all the Commonwealth realms.

THE CARIBBEAN

The Caribbean includes Her Majesty's realms – countries in which she is both monarch and head of state – of Barbados, Jamaica, Antigua and Barbuda, Belize, St Kitts and Nevis, St Vincent and the Grenadines, Grenada, St Lucia and the Bahamas. The Caribbean region also covers British Overseas Territories. These are still under British jurisdiction, and include Bermuda, Montserrat, the British Virgin Islands, the Cayman Islands, the Turks and Caicos Islands and Anguilla.

Some countries in the region have moved to sever

links with the Crown. For example, Guyana dropped the Queen as head of state in 1970 and Trinidad and Tobago followed suit in 1976, although both opted to remain in the Commonwealth. Nevertheless, the Queen has described the Caribbean region as 'a miniature version of the Commonwealth', saying that she has always had a deep affection for its diversity and vibrancy.

NON-COMMONWEALTH COUNTRIES
THE VATICAN CITY

In October 1980, the Pope welcomed the Queen, who was dressed in a long black gown in line with protocol, to the Vatican City. This visit to the Vatican was seen as a big step towards strengthening relations between the Church of England and the Roman Catholic Church. Two years later, the Queen returned the compliment, welcoming John Paul II at Buckingham Palace – the first papal visit to Britain for 450 years.

CHINA

In October 1986, the Queen became the first British monarch to visit China. It was seen as a hugely significant and successful diplomatic mission. However, the tour was nearly upset by the media's focus on Prince Philip's infamous comment that British students might become 'slitty-eyed' if they stayed in China much longer. However, although the British press went into overdrive, the Queen's hosts were seemingly unmoved.

USA

The Queen sealed the special relationship with the USA on a state visit in 1991. In the first address to the US Congress by a British monarch, she celebrated the cooperation and unity between the two countries, saying, 'Some people believe that power grows from the barrel of a gun. So it can, but history shows that it never grows well, or for very long. Force, in the end, is sterile. We have gone a better way: our societies rest on mutual agreement, on contract and on consensus.'

RUSSIA

The Queen visited Russia for the first time in 1994, the first British monarch to have set foot on the country's soil. (In 1908, Edward VII got as far as sailing into Russian waters for lunch with the Tsar.) She toured Moscow and St Petersburg and, at the Kremlin, exchanged gifts with President Boris Yeltsin. They discussed problems of corruption and violence facing the new Russia and she listened as he told her how difficult it would be to establish a decent government. Her visit was one of the key episodes in relations between post-Soviet Russia

President and Mrs. Bush host a state dinner for the Queen and Prince Philip at the White House, May 1991. (PD)

and the UK, and was aimed at strengthening economic, political and cultural ties between the two countries. President Yeltsin regarded the Queen's visit as a sign of recognition of his democratic achievements by the Western democratic states.

EUROPE
MALTA

Malta is the only other country outside the UK that the Queen has called home; she lived there on and off between 1949 and 1951 when she was dividing her time between her naval officer husband, Prince Philip, who had been posted to the island, and her baby son in the care of nannies back home. In Malta, Princess Elizabeth was able to live in much the same way as any other navy wife, albeit in a grander house. As such, she was spotted driving her MG car, dining at local restaurants, visiting the hair salon, shopping with friends and attending dances. It is thought to be the closest experience she has ever had to normal life.

She returned to Malta in 1954, on the way home from her first grand world tour as monarch, stopping there for a few days to board the new Royal Yacht Britannia. The island became a republic in 1974. Nevertheless, in November 2007, the Queen and Prince Philip chose to spend their 60th wedding anniversary there, while en route to Uganda for the CHOGM.

CYPRUS

The island state of Cyprus joined the Commonwealth in 1960 on gaining independence, when it became the Republic of Cyprus. After then, tensions rose between the Greek Cypriot and Turkish Cypriot communities on the island. In 1974, after a Greek military coup, Cyprus was invaded by Turkish troops who partitioned the island, occupying the northern part. The United Nations-monitored Green Line still divides the two territories. The Commonwealth has long protested about the occupation and tried to resolve it through negotiation. The Queen visited Cyprus in 1983 and 1984. In 1993, she spent a week there before the CHOGM.

WEST GERMANY

The Queen toured Germany in May 1965. This, her first visit, lasted 11 days and took in 18 cities. The trip was seen as a major contribution to healing the wounds caused by World War II and was the first visit to Germany by a British monarch in more than half a century. The Queen made a speech to a vast crowd in which she referred to her German ancestry and the links between Britain and West Berlin. She returned for a much shorter visit in 1978 and again in 1987. In 1990, after the fall of the Berlin Wall, she visited once more at the invitation of President Richard von Weizsäcker. In June 2015 the Queen made one of her last overseas visits to Germany.

THE MONARCH
AND POLITICS

THE QUEEN IN PARLIAMENT

The formal phrase 'Queen in Parliament' is used to describe the British legislature, which consists of the sovereign, the House of Lords and the House of Commons. The monarch's duties include officially opening each new session of Parliament, granting royal assent to legislation, and approving Orders and Proclamations through the Privy Council. The Queen also has a special relationship with the prime minister, retaining the right to appoint one and also meeting him or her by granting an Audience on a regular basis. In addition to playing a specific role in the UK Parliament based in London, the Queen has formal roles with relation to the devolved assemblies of Scotland, Wales and Northern Ireland.

The Queen's prime ministers

Fourteen British prime ministers have served the Queen during her reign, the first of whom was Sir Winston Churchill. Throughout her reign, Elizabeth has held weekly Audiences in the form of one-to-one meetings with her sitting prime minister, in order to discuss government matters. The Audience is usually held in an Audience Room in Her Majesty's apartments and is entirely private. While a monarch remains politically neutral on all matters they have the right to 'be consulted, advise and warn' ministers, including her prime minister, when necessary.

Furthermore, when a potential prime minister is called to Buckingham Palace following a general election or a resignation, he or she will travel to Buckingham Palace for a special Audience during which the sovereign will ask whether he or she will form a government. The most usual response is acceptance. In addition, before the Budget is presented to Parliament, the Chancellor of the Exchequer has an Audience with the monarch.

Although the Audiences are supposed to be strictly confidential, former Labour Prime Minister Tony Blair did reveal during the BBC documentary *Queen & Country* in 2002 that Elizabeth brought him back down to earth the morning he became prime minister by reminding him of his relative youth and inexperience of government. Recalling the meeting on 2 May 1997, at which she formally invited him to form a new government, he said, 'She did say to me that Winston Churchill was the first prime minister that she dealt with, and that was before I was born. So I got a sense of my, er, my relative seniority, or lack of it.' Mr Blair was 43 at the time.

The Queen's speech from the throne in the State Opening of Parliament. Seated to the right of the Queen, is the young Prince Charles, the Duke of Edinburgh sits next to the Queen, with Princess Anne seated on his left. Holding the Great Sword of State, Field Marshal Viscount Montgomery of Alamein (right), at left Lord Shackleton with the Cap of Maintenance. (PA Images)

Winston Churchill with the Queen, Prince Charles and Princess Anne, in 1953. (PD)

Mr Blair also said that he has shared innermost thoughts with the Queen: 'There are only two people in the world frankly to whom a prime minister can say what he likes about Cabinet colleagues. One's the wife, and the other's the Queen.' He added: 'She [the Queen] is about the only person that you can tell something to in complete confidence and know that the confidence will never be broken. And I've done that on several occasions.'

Appointing a prime minister

As long as Britain retains the first-past-the-post single member constituency system for electing members of Parliament, the monarch's job of appointing a new prime minister is relatively simple: she must offer the job to whoever is most likely to command a majority in the House of Commons. Within hours of a general election result, therefore, the monarch invites the leader of the party that has returned the most Members of Parliament to become prime minister and to form a government.

In the case of a prime minister resigning mid-term, they can advise the Queen about who they think the successor should be, although, technically, she is not obliged to take the advice.

All of this means that the monarch now plays a passive role, one that is almost entirely symbolic, when in comes to 'choosing' the prime minister.

THE CHANGEOVER PROCESS

The rules on how the changeover of one prime minister to another will happen is partly due to unwritten constitution of the UK, partly hidebound tradition and partly up to those involved.

Usually, the outgoing prime minister will make the short journey to Buckingham Palace to see the Queen and tender his or her resignation as Prime Minister and First Lord of the Treasury. The relaxed meeting usually lasts no more than 20 minutes before the outgoing premier leaves, no longer with the trappings of state, such as the chauffeur-driven car.

Soon after, the new leader of the party that can command a majority in the House of Commons will go to the palace to, as they say, 'kiss hands' and the Queen invites him or her to become her prime minister. What happens between them is kept private.

The Queen at 10 Downing Street, January 1985, to celebrate 250 years of it being the official residence of the British Prime Minister, with leaders past and present (l to r) James Callaghan, Sir Alec Douglas-Home, Margaret Thatcher, Harold Macmillan, Harold Wilson and Ted Heath. (PA Images)

CONTENTIOUS CHOICES

Despite the fact that technically she has now no say in who becomes prime minister, the Queen became embroiled in a political controversy over her selection – after seeking advice – of a prime minister in 1957 and again in 1963. Both times involved senior Conservative Minister Richard A. Butler, affectionately known as 'Rab', who twice failed to become Conservative party leader and consequently prime minister, losing out to Harold Macmillan in 1957 and Alec Douglas-Home in 1963.

This was partly because Butler's consensual Toryism was viewed with suspicion by some party members, but also because he was deemed to lack the ultimate ambition and ruthlessness to seize the opportunity presented to him. His first chance came in 1957 when Prime Minister Anthony Eden resigned due to ill health. Butler was seen among Tory MPs as the popular choice, but the young Queen, who had only been on the throne for five years, wavered and sought the counsel of Tory peers Lord Salisbury and Lord Kilmuir, who advised her that the majority of support was for Old Etonian Harold Macmillan. The latter was summoned to the Palace and invited to be prime minister, which he duly accepted.

In 1963, when MacMillan also quit the post due to ill health – so ill in fact that the Queen had to go to his hospital bed in order for him to resign – Butler was seen by many as the natural choice. Macmillan did not favour him, however, and advised the Queen that the 14th Earl of Home – an improbable choice – should take his place. The Queen took no other soundings. Earl Home duly renounced his aristocratic title, found a safe seat for a by-election and entered the House of Commons as prime minister as Alec Douglas-Home. His was a short-lived premiership, however, since he served for just a year before he lost the general election to Labour's Harold Wilson. Butler, meanwhile, whose failure to land the top job led to him being dubbed 'The Best Prime Minister That Britain Never Had', became a life peer in 1965 and died on 8 March 1982.

A NOTE ON KISSING

The term 'kissing of hands' is a relic of the days when a monarch still called many cabinet-making shots; these days there is no actual kissing of hands. The prime minister will be announced as he or she enters the room and will bow or curtsey to the monarch. The only kissing that takes place occurs when a member of the Privy Council is appointed, in which instance he or she kneels on a footstool in front of the Queen, who proffers her right hand, palm downwards with fingers lightly closed. The new privy counsellor or minister then extends his or her right hand, palm upwards and, taking the monarch's hand lightly, will kiss it with no more than a touch of the lips.

In the past, however, Benjamin Disraeli used the opportunity of a kiss to declare to Queen Victoria on their first meeting his 'loving loyalty and faith.' By contrast, Labour left stalwart the late Tony Benn revealed in his diaries that he put his thumb out and kissed his own thumb when he was inducted into the Privy Council. Republican, and once Labour Leader of the Opposition, Jeremy Corbyn MP let it be known that he didn't want to kneel before the Queen when he too was inducted into the Privy Council, and she didn't insist.

THE QUEEN'S ROLE IN THE CONSTITUTION

Politics in Great Britain takes place within the framework of a constitutional monarchy and parliamentary democracy in which the monarch, currently Queen Elizabeth II, is head of state, and the prime minister is the head of the United Kingdom government and the leader of her Cabinet of Secretaries of State.

There is no single set of rules of government, known as a constitution, though it is often said that the UK's constitution it unwritten. In reality, most of it is written but not in one single formal document. Instead, it is formed from various sources, including statute law, case law made by judges, international treaties, as well as unwritten sources, including parliamentary conventions and royal prerogatives.

Parliament and the Crown

Parliament is highest legislative authority in the UK. It is made up of the House of Commons, House of Lords and the hereditary monarch. The Crown, another way of referring to the monarchy, is the oldest part of the system. The monarch's power has been greatly reduced over time: today, it is largely ceremonial, involved in events such as the State of Opening of Parliament.

OPENING AND DISSOLVING PARLIAMENT

The monarch opens Parliament by means of the State Opening, which marks the beginning of the Parliamentary year. Since the Fixed-term Parliaments Act 2011, the monarch can dissolve Parliament only before a general election, under conditions laid out in the Act (see opposite). In reality, the decision lies with the sitting prime minister even though the law says otherwise. However, as Prime Minister Boris Johnson discovered in September 2019, he can only succeed in getting a general election with the support of two-thirds of the MPs in Parliament. If the opposition MPs combine with rebels and other parties, then they can frustrate the government's plans to dissolve Parliament, which is exactly what happened when MPs turned down Boris Johnson's motion for a general election. After the historic Commons vote, Johnson said that the leader of the opposition, Jeremy Corbyn, was the first in British history to 'refuse the invitation to an election'.

THE QUEEN'S SPEECH

The Queen's Speech contains an outline of proposed legislation and government policies for the new parliamentary session. Although the monarch reads

Did you know?

Legally the Queen is entitled to vote in UK elections, but because as head of state she must remain politically neutral, she declines to do so. By convention, other members of the royal family do not vote either, owing to their closeness to the monarch.

THE FIXED-TERM PARLIAMENTS ACT

Before the 2011 Fixed-term Parliaments Act, the power to dissolve Parliament was one of the prerogative powers that the prime minister could exercise on behalf of the Crown. In 2011, however, the Act was passed in a bid to take the politics out of the dissolution of Parliament. It was part of the then coalition government's constitutional reform agenda. Nick Clegg, leader of the Liberal Democratic Party, and then deputy prime minister, said that the Bill had: 'A single, clear purpose: to introduce fixed-term Parliaments to the United Kingdom to remove the right of a prime minister to seek the Dissolution of Parliament for pure political gain' and thereby avoid snap elections. It provided for five-year parliaments as a norm. The only exception would be an 'early election' under section 2 of the Act. This would apply in two cases:

1. If the House of Commons passed a motion that, 'there shall be an early parliamentary general election' with a majority of at least two-thirds.
2. A vote of no confidence by MPs that was not reversed in 14 days.

In reality, a prime minister with a good majority in the House of Commons can still call a snap election with the only objective of making that majority bigger. Many experts believe this piece of constitutional tinkering has failed to achieve its objective, as shown by Prime Minister Theresa May's ability to call a general election in 2017 when the Conservatives had a 21 per cent rating in the polls. It was also widely criticised in 2019 and even blamed for leading to the political impasse over Brexit in September 2019. Leader of the House of Commons in 2019 Jacob Rees-Mogg described it as a 'monstrosity' and said the hastily drafted legislation had prevented Mr Johnson from calling a general election to break the deadlock because it requires the agreement of two thirds of MPs.

THE ROYAL PREROGATIVE

The royal prerogative is a key part of the UK's unwritten constitution that dates back to medieval monarchs acting as head of the kingdom. Today, the majority of royal prerogatives are no longer in the hands of the monarch but are instead used by the executive arm of government. The powers technically give the sovereign the ability to declare war, to appoint a prime minster and to dissolve Parliament, but since the Fixed-term Parliaments Act 2011 the monarch can dissolve Parliament only under the terms laid out by the Act. However, the Queen does have some control over the appointment of ministers: 'the Queen has unlimited power to appoint whom she pleases to be her ministers'. The representatives of the Crown are usually ministers who form part of the executive. They are directly responsible to Parliament when exercising the powers of the royal prerogative.

The royal prerogatives can be categorised into quite a number of different areas, one of the most important of which is judicial. Others range from the signing of treaties, which is usually done by a minister on behalf of the Queen, to the opening of Parliament – one of the few royal prerogatives the Queen still exercises herself. There is no clear definition as to the extent to which these powers exist and whether or not some of these prerogatives are still viable today; some, such as the power to press men into the navy, have fallen out of use altogether, probably forever.

it personally from the throne of the House of Lords, it is written by the government. As soon as the monarch leaves, a new parliamentary session starts and Parliament gets back to work. MPs then debate the speech and agree an 'Address in Reply to Her Majesty's Gracious Speech'.

ROYAL ASSENT

Every piece of legislation enacted by Parliament needs royal assent to become law, which means the monarch must agree to it. When a bill has been approved by a majority in the House of Commons and the House of Lords, it is therefore formally agreed to by the Crown. This turns a bill into an Act of Parliament, allowing it to become law in the UK. The present Queen has never refused royal assent during her reign. The last monarch to consider withholding royal assent was George V, who had serious reservations over the Irish Home Rule Bill 1914 to establish a separate Parliament in Dublin that would be subsidiary to Westminster. The outbreak of World War I put the issue on the back burner, suspending its progress.

The Privy Council

The Privy Council goes back to the earliest days of the monarchy and was once appointed by the sovereign to advise on matters of state. In today's constitutional monarchy, the monarch acts on the advice of his or her government ministers, so the Privy Council over time has had to adapt. A Privy Counsellor must swear to be a 'true and faithful servant' to the Crown, to 'bear faith and allegiance' to the monarch's 'majesty' and to 'keep secret all matters committed and revealed ... in Council'.

The Privy Council still meets regularly, on average once a month, but its business is transacted in discussion and correspondence between its ministerial members and the government departments that advise them. It has been commonplace for prime ministers to share information, some of it classified, with leaders of the opposition on 'Privy Council terms', on the express understanding that it will not be made public or divulged in any way. This is because one section of the oath states: 'You will keep secret all Matters committed unto you.'

Judicial Committee of the Privy Council hosted in Middlesex Guildhall in London. (ChrisVGT Photography CC)

CONSTITUTIONAL CRISES

A constitutional crisis is a conflict in the function of a government that the political constitution is seen as incapable of resolving. In Britain, the first one came with the regency crisis of 1788. That year, a new Parliament convened while George III was unable, due to illness, to charge it with its responsibilities or assent to any bills. Parliament responded by submitting a bill that provided for the Prince of Wales to act as Prince Regent. It was repeated in 1811 when the king again fell ill.

Another crisis occurred when the Liberal government's so-called 'People's Budget' of 1909–10 introduced unprecedented taxes on the lands and incomes of Britain's wealthy to fund new social welfare programmes. It was passed in the House of Commons in 1909, but the issue spiralled and when George V inherited the throne he was faced with one the most testing domestic challenges of any monarch in recent history. When in 1910–11 the Tory-dominated House of Lords overturned the Liberal government's legislation, it triggered a constitutional crisis and a two-year impasse before the Parliament Act 1911 was introduced, depriving the Upper Chamber of its absolute power of veto on legislation. It was followed in 1913–14 with the furious controversy over Irish home rule, which many feared could end in civil war.

Another major crisis occurred in 1936 when King Edward VIII proposed to marry twice-divorced Wallis Simpson against the advice of his ministers. This led to Edward effectively being forced to give up the throne to avoid a constitutional crisis.

Avoiding conflict

The Queen has always done her best to be seen to be politically neutral in public, thus avoiding a clash with the sitting government that acts in her name. Many believe that her successor, Prince Charles, will find it difficult to emulate his mother. Critics of the monarchy such as republicans, or staunch traditionalists, argue that Prince Charles has and is repeatedly operating dangerously outside of his constitutional remit.

The anti-monarchists' view is that any king or queen regnant (or heir apparent, for that matter) must not be in any way political or partisan as that would leave them and the system exposed. It is true that the overwhelming majority of prerogative powers are devolved to the sovereign's ministers, but the monarch can wield power in the event of what he or she perceives is 'a grave

Prince Charles faces the press during a walkabout on a Foreign Office sponsored visit to Bahrain and the Middle East in November 2016. The tour was designed to strengthen the United Kingdom's warm bilateral relations with key partners in the region. But UK MPs said there was 'plainly a perception' that the issue of human rights had been downgraded in the government's dealings with countries such as Saudi Arabia, Egypt and Bahrain ahead of the visit. (Jobson Media)

constitutional crisis', in which case the sovereign can act 'contrary to or without ministerial advice'.

Prince Charles, though, has a very different take on it. 'I don't see why politicians and others should think they have the monopoly of wisdom', he said during an interview with his biographer Jonathan Dimbleby in 1994 when asked about his involvement in politics. However, in a more recent BBC documentary to mark his 70th birthday in 2018, the prince sought to quell concerns that he would be a 'meddling' or activist king, saying 'I'm not that stupid.' Declaring the role of sovereign and heir to be different, he stated that he was aware of the constraints he will encounter as king, and claimed that his behaviour will change. 'It is vital to remember there's only room for one sovereign at a time. Not two', he said. 'You can't be the same as the sovereign if you're the Prince of Wales or the heir. But the idea somehow that I'm going to go on in exactly the same way if I have to succeed is complete nonsense because the two situations are completely different.'

> ## Did you know?
> Prince Philip once said, 'If the people of this country want a republic, that's a perfectly viable alternative.'

FINANCING AND WEALTH

HOW THE QUEEN IS FUNDED

It is often stated that the Queen is one of the richest individual in the world. That statement is way off the mark. The truth is she is not even close to being the richest aristocrat in Britain. She is actually worth around £440 million – a sizeable fortune, of course, but one that is dwarfed by the Duke of Westminster's near £10 billion fortune or the £6.7 billion of the Earl of Cadogan and his family.

There is also a distinct difference between what the Queen receives from the government to fund the monarchy and her personal wealth. The former amount is fairly transparent, whereas her private wealth remains private and can only be guessed at. It should also be noted that that estimated figure doesn't include the priceless works of art in the Royal Collection or the palaces, because technically these do not belong to her but to the country.

The Queen's private wealth

Estimations of the Queen's current private wealth are based on previous calculations rather than any formal divulgence, and vary:

- In 1971, the Queen's former private secretary, Sir Jock Colville, and a director of her bank, Coutts, estimated her wealth to be £2 million – the equivalent of about £28 million today.
- In 1993, an official statement from Buckingham Palace called estimates of £100 million 'grossly overstated'.
- In 2002, the Queen inherited her mother's estate, thought to have been worth £70 million – the equivalent of about £112 million today.
- In 2011, *Forbes* magazine estimated the Queen's net worth at about £325 million, whereas in 2012 *The Sunday Times* placed it at £310 million.
- In 2015, an analysis by the Bloomberg Billionaires Index put it at about £275 million.

Did you know?
According to experts, the monarchy contributes around £1.8 billion to the UK economy annually, including £550 million that is directly generated by tourism.

Did you know?
The Queen rarely carries money on her person. The only exception is a £5 note, folded into a little square so you can only see her face, that she carries to church on Sunday in order to make her offering contribution.

The Crown's wealth

Historically, the wealth of the Crown flowed from inherited properties acquired through centuries of conquest, forfeiture and purchases. Indeed, the practice of establishing Crown lands – or land belonging to the monarch – dates all the way back to the Norman conquest.

Different kings and queens have gained and lost land over the years, as the cost of governance grew over time. Furthermore, when George III took the throne in 1760, the way in which royal finances were managed underwent a major change. Parliament began to pay for the entirety of the 'Civil List' government expenditures and Royal Household costs, which had been traditionally handled by the monarch. In exchange, Parliament would receive the hereditary revenues of the Crown Estate.While the Crown Estate is owned by the monarch for the duration of their reign, it is not their private property and cannot be sold by the monarch, nor do revenues from it belong to the monarch.

Sovereign Grant

This is the allowance provided annually by the UK government to support the Queen in her official duties. It was calculated that the grant cost each British taxpayer 69 pence in 2018, which led to courtiers insisting that the royal family is good value for money.

The Sovereign Grant replaced the Civil List in 2011 when the Sovereign Grant Act was given royal assent on 18 October that year. This meant that on 1 April 2012, the arrangements for the funding of the Queen's official duties changed.

The new system simplified the monarchy's funding, replacing the Civil List and the three Grants-in-Aid (for royal travel, communications and information, and the maintenance of the Royal Palaces) with a single, consolidated annual grant. It was introduced to be a

more permanent arrangement than the old Civil List system, which was specific to the reign.

Funding for the Sovereign Grant is procured as a percentage (initially set at 15 per cent) of the profits of the Crown Estate revenue. Annual financial accounts are prepared and published by the keeper of the privy purse, and the grant is reviewed every five years by the Royal Trustees – the prime minister, the Chancellor of the Exchequer and the keeper of the privy purse. This means that the Royal Household is subject to the same audit scrutiny as other government expenditure, via the National Audit Office and the Public Accounts Committee. Furthermore, the Royal Household has committed to spend public money as wisely and efficiently as possible and to making royal finances transparent and comprehensible.

The Sovereign Grant Act 2011 effectively abolished all parliamentary annuities other than the annual payment received by Prince Philip. Subsequently, the living costs of the members of the royal family who carry out official duties, including Prince Andrew, Prince Edward and Countess of Wessex, and Princess Anne, are now mainly met through the Queen's income from the Duchy of Lancaster. This excludes security expenses.

Hannah Belcher from the Royal Collection Trust Exhibitions team applies the finishing touches to the Grand Service commissioned by George IV, part of a Christmas display in the State Dining Room at Windsor Castle, November 2014. The Royal Collection is made up of over one million objects, spread over 13 royal residences. (PA Images)

EXPENDITURE IN 2018/19

Each year, the Royal Household publishes a summary of head of state expenditure, together with a full report on royal public finances. These records show the following:

♛ *The Queen was given £82.2 million to support her official duties in 2018/19, up from £76.1 million the year before. Half of the cash went on the upkeep of Buckingham Palace and other royal residences, reflecting the age and national importance of the buildings.*
♛ *The cost of royal travel fell by £100,000 to £4.6 million.*

♛ *Five big tours saw the Royal Household's carbon emissions double.*
♛ *The Queen and other royals spent almost £200,000 on private jets for travel to and from Scotland.*

The current keeper of the privy purse, Sir Michael Stevens, who is in charge of the Queen's accounts, said the report showed that she continued to be highly active, conducting 140 engagements in 12 months. The wider family undertook more than 3,200 official duties in the UK and abroad.

HOW PRINCE CHARLES IS FUNDED

The Oval, home ground of Surrey Cricket Ground, is an asset owned by the Duchy of Cornwall. Surrey County Cricket Club became the sole leaseholder of the ground in 1874. (Shutterstock)

Prince Charles is funded by the Duchy of Cornwall. This is a private estate that was established by Edward III in 1337 to provide independence to his son and heir, Prince Edward. A charter ruled that each future Duke of Cornwall would be the eldest surviving son of the monarch and heir to the throne. The revenue from his estate is used to fund the public, private and charitable activities of the Duke and his children.

Charles's income from the Duchy of Cornwall in 2018/2019 was £21.6 million. He funded his wife and sons' households from this. Charles pays income tax on the surplus, after official expenditure has been deducted, at the highest rate, (45 per cent in 2016–17). This resulted in a total tax bill of £4.8 million. The estate comprises arable and livestock farms, residential and commercial properties, forests, rivers, quarries and coastline. It extends beyond Cornwall, covering 52,760 hectares of land. Under the guidance of the Duke of Cornwall, it is the Duchy's responsibility to manage the estate in a manner that is sustainable, financially viable and of value to the local community.

Prince Charles spends the majority of his after-tax income supporting his and Camilla's working activities and those of the Duke and Duchess of Cambridge and the Duke and Duchess of Sussex. The income also funds his personal spending. Public money is used to aid the Prince and the Duchess in specific areas in supporting the Queen as head of state, including the costs incurred for security; travel costs when they fly or go by train to and from official engagements; and property maintenance on royal residences. These and other other financial figures are published every year in the Annual Review published by Charles's office.

In November 2017 the Queen gave permission for Harry and Meghan to base their Household Office at Buckingham Palace. This meant that the expenses were divided, not necessarily equally, between the Prince of Wales and the Queen. Privately, Prince Charles's worth is estimated at just over £1 billion. He owns land and property across 23 English and Welsh counties.

COMMON Q&AS

Q) WHY DOESN'T THE DUCHY OF CORNWALL PAY CORPORATION TAX?
A) *The Duchy is not a company and is therefore not liable to pay corporation tax. Charles is also not entitled to receive any capital gains from the Duchy, and therefore does not pay capital gains tax. He does pay capital gains tax, however, on any other capital gains he may receive from any other sources.*

Q) HOW ARE PRINCE CHARLES AND THE DUCHESS OF CORNWALL'S OFFICIAL ACTIVITIES FUNDED?
A) *Most of Charles and Camilla's public activities are paid for from his income from the Duchy of Cornwall.*

OTHER REVENUE STREAMS

The Crown Estate

The Crown Estate is a collection of lands and holdings in the UK that belongs to the British monarch as a corporation sole, making it the 'Sovereign's public estate'. It is neither government property nor part of the monarch's private estate.

The Sovereign Grant, which funds the Queen, is 15 per cent of the annual profit of the Crown Estate. This figure can be increased in exceptional circumstances. In 2015, for instance, it was announced that the amount would be increased to 25 per cent in order to pay for essential renovations to Buckingham Palace. The Sovereign Grant, however, cannot decrease from the previous year, even if the Crown Estate is less profitable. The National Audit Office has free rein to audit the Grant.

Parliamentary annuities

Despite retiring from public duties in 2017 the Duke of Edinburgh still receives a parliamentary annuity of £359,000 per year direct from the Treasury. This goes towards funding his private office. In the past, some other members of the British royal family also

THE PARADISE PAPERS

In 2017 the so-called 'Paradise Papers' revealed that the Duchy held investments in two offshore financial centres: the Cayman Islands and Bermuda. Both are British Overseas Territories of which the Queen is monarch. Labour Party Leader Jeremy Corbyn insisted that the Queen should apologise, saying anyone with money offshore for tax avoidance should 'not just apologise for it, [but] recognise what it does to our society'. A spokesman for the Duchy responded by saying that all of their investments are audited and legitimate and that the Queen voluntarily pays taxes on income she receives from Duchy investments.

received funding in the form of parliamentary annuities. For example, the Civil List Act 1952 provided for an allowance for the Queen's sister, the late Princess Margaret, as well as allowances to the Queen's younger children, among others.

The Civil List Act 1972 added further members of the royal family to the annuity list. By 2002, there were eight recipients, all children or first cousins of the Queen. Between them, they received £1.5 million annually. Between 1993 and 2012, the Queen voluntarily refunded the cost of these payments to the Treasury.

The Duchy of Lancaster

The Duchy of Lancaster is a body responsible for managing an investment portfolio of land, property and financial investments. It was created under Charter in 1399 and its main purpose is to provide an income for the sovereign as Duke of Lancaster. The sovereign is not entitled to any of the capital assets of the Duchy. The Queen as sovereign is the current Duke of Lancaster. In the financial year ending 31 March 2018, the estate was valued at about £534 million. The net income of the Duchy amounts to about £20 million per year.

CHANCELLOR OF THE DUCHY OF LANCASTER

The chancellor of the Duchy of Lancaster is a ministerial office in the government of the UK that includes as part of its duties the administration of the estates and rents of the Duchy. The chancellor of the Duchy of Lancaster is appointed by the sovereign on the advice of the prime minister and is answerable to Parliament for the governance of the Duchy. He or she has responsibility for advising the prime minister on policy implementation, and management of Cabinet committees.

Left: Aerial view of Lancaster Castle. (Shutterstock)

TAXATION AND THE CROWN

The Crown is legally exempt from paying tax because certain acts of Parliament do not apply to it. Crown bodies such as the Duchy of Lancaster are therefore not subject to legislation concerning income tax, capital gains tax or inheritance tax. The sovereign has no legal liability to pay such taxes. The Duchy of Cornwall has a Crown exemption and Prince Charles is not legally liable to pay income tax on Duchy revenues.

A 'Memorandum of Understanding on Royal Taxation' was first published on 5 February 1993 and subsequently amended in 1996, 2009 and 2013. The intention is that the arrangements stipulated in the memorandum will be followed by the next monarch. It details the private arrangements by which the Queen and Prince Charles make voluntary payments to HM Revenue and Customs in lieu of tax to compensate for their tax exemption status.

For example, the Queen voluntarily pays a sum equivalent to income tax on both her private income and any income from the Privy Purse (including the Duchy of Lancaster) that is not used for official

purposes. Monies from the Sovereign Grant are exempted from this calculation. A sum equivalent to capital gains tax is also voluntarily paid on any gains from the disposal of private assets made after 5 April 1993.

Arrangements also exist for a sum in lieu of inheritance tax to be paid on some of the Queen's private assets. This does not apply to property passing from monarch to monarch, nor to property passing from the consort of a former monarch to the current monarch.

Prince Charles also makes voluntary payments. Today, these include a sum equivalent to income tax on the income from the Duchy of Cornwall that is in excess of what is needed to meet official expenditure. From 1969–81, the voluntary tax payments amounted to 50 per cent of the Duchy profits, a figure that was reduced to 25 per cent in 1981 when Charles married Lady Diana Spencer. This arrangement was eventually replaced by the memorandum in 1993. The income of Prince Charles from sources other than the Duchy of Cornwall is subject to tax in the normal way.

A view inside the non-private residence hall of Prince Charles and the Duchess of Cornwall's property in Llwynywermod, Wales. (PA Images)

THE ROYAL MINT

Following the withdrawal of the Romans from Britain around AD410, it seems that no coins were struck in Britain for some 200 years. After the consolidation of the English Kingdoms around AD650 the use of coinage in the form of the silver penny re-emerged and a London mint was in operation, albeit in a somewhat precarious fashion. By the time of Alfred the Great (871–99), however, its history had become continuous and increasingly important, and many more mints sprang up, mostly in the south of England. By the time of Ethelred II (978–1016) it is thought there were 70.

From then until the early 13th century, the number of mints is thought to have declined to just a few, mostly in and around London and Canterbury, although it is not known exactly where the London mint was located. This changed in 1279 when a single mint, under the direct control of the monarch, was formed within the Tower of London, where it was based for the next 500 years. In 1812, a new mint was built at Tower Hill. In 1966, when decimalisation was announced, it was agreed that it would relocate to Llantrisant near Cardiff, Wales, to upsize and cope with the demands of recoinage. In 2009, following recommendations for it to be privatized, the Royal Mint stopped being a government agency and became a state company owned by HM Treasury.

Coins, currency and royalty

In the 500 years prior to 1280, silver pennies were the only royal coins in circulation in England. These commonly carried the name of the king for whom they were struck. After 1280, however, a range of denominations began to emerge, and in the mid-14th century a regular coinage of gold was introduced.

In 1489, under King Henry VII, the gold sovereign came into existence, featuring an image of the monarch's head. The purpose of this was both practical and for propaganda: having an image of the king's head on the coin would have made him known to all classes of his subjects. Henry VII also created a currency that was trusted across the world.

In the early 19th century UK coin production was streamlined, powered by the Industrial Revolution. This resulted in a shift that saw coins being produced by machine. This was facilitated by the relocation of the Royal Mint to the new premises on Tower Hill, where there were new steam-powered coining presses. Further changes took place in the 1960s, when the Mint moved to modern premises at Llantrisant, Wales.

Royal face off

Even after a thousand years and many changes in production techniques, the monarch's image continues to be shown on the obverse of modern UK coins.

The design of British coins goes back to the reign of Charles II, when it was stipulated that the direction the head of the featured monarch should face either left or right alternately between the coins of successive monarchs. So if a predecessor faced left ,the next monarch would face right. The exception to this was the limited coinage minted during the brief reign of Edward VIII, who insisted his likeness faced left. It is for this reason that the profile of the Queen faces right on coins but left on stamps. The presence of images of the monarch on bank notes is a recent practice. The Queen is the only monarch whose face has appeared on bank notes, as the custom only started in 1960

Workers at the Royal Mint, London, examine the finished coins on an overlooking machine and remove any coins that have tiny defects, July 1949. (PA Images).

FIVE QUEEN'S HEADS

During Elizabeth II's reign there have been five representations of the Queen on circulating coinage:

1. *The original coin portrait of Elizabeth was by Mary Gillick and was adopted at the beginning of the Queen's reign in 1952.*
2. *The second effigy was by Arnold Machin, approved in 1964. That portrait was used on all the decimal coins from 1968.*
3. *The next effigy was by Raphael Maklouf and was adopted in 1985.*
4. *The fourth, introduced in 1998, was by Ian Rank-Broadley.*
5. *The latest portrait was introduced in 2015, and is by Jody Clark.*

STAMPS

The current postal system in the UK has its basis in the service that was set up many hundreds of years ago to quickly convey court documents around the country.

These letters – pertaining to affairs of state and despatches in times of war – were carried by special messengers of the court employed for particular occasions. Speed was often of the essences, so, to facilitate this service, Henry VIII's 'Master of the Posts' set up post-stages along the major roads of the kingdom where royal couriers could change horses and so continue their journey as quickly as possible.

During this extended period there were four posts around the country:

1. The Courte to Barwicke (from the court to Scotland)
2. The Courte to Beaumoris (from the court to Ireland)
3. The Courte to Dover (from the court to Europe)
4. The Courte to Plymouth (from the court to the Royal Dockyard)

Right: Sheets of the famous Penny Black (r), Two-Penny Blues and One-Penny Reds stamps. Featuring the head of Queen Victoria, these were the world's first adhesive postage stamp, first issued in May 1840. (PA Images)

Five special commemorative stamps featuring classic portraits of the Queen, are held outside Buckingham Palace. The stamps were issued by Royal Mail on 6 February 2002, exactly 50 years after her accession to the throne. (PA Images)

To raise funds, Charles I later opened these posts to public use, although court letters constituted the majority of the mail. What's more, as late as 1807 court missives coming into London were, unlike ordinary letters, delivered the moment the mail arrived.

The postal system rapidly spread during the reign of Queen Victoria with the introduction of the Uniform Penny Post in 1840 (see below), and the Queen's letters bore postage stamps like everyone else's. However, royal messengers continued to carry certain letters by hand. Special postal facilities, in the form of a court post office, were also established under Queen Victoria – something that is still in use today.

A royal hangover

Despite becoming a public service nearly 200 years ago, the postal system still retains various royal connections:

- A miniature silhouette of the monarch's head is depicted on all stamps.
- The personal cyphers of the Queen or her predecessors appear on most letterboxes.
- The main postal delivery service is known as the Royal Mail.

The image of the Queen, which appears on UK postage stamps, was designed by Arnold Machin, who originally created it as a sculpture. Issued on 5 June 1967, it has remained unchanged for four decades. The Queen is shown facing left, wearing the Diamond Diadem, as she does when travelling to the State Opening of Parliament.

Royal Philatelic Collection

George V was an avid collector and was determined to have the best collection of British Empire stamps anywhere. To this end, he dedicated significant financial resources to it.

A number of the rare stamps in the collection were also given to the monarch of the day, such as stamps that were withdrawn before issue, and preproduction material, such as proofs and essays. Experts estimate that the collection, which is privately owned by the Queen, is worth more than £30 million, if not more. The most valuable stamp in the collection, the 2d Mauritius 'Post Office' of 1847, is valued at £2 million.

THE UNIFORM PENNY POST

This government initiative changed the way the Royal Mail worked in the 19th century, making it a government monopoly, standardising it and removing the scope for abuse that had previously been rife. A simple scheme, it meant that anybody could send a letter between two places in the UK for a fixed price of one penny.

Did you know?

The Arnold Machin image of the Queen is the most reproduced work of art in history, with over 200 billion examples produced so far.

ROYAL
RESIDENCES

BUCKINGHAM PALACE

An early morning view of the front of Buckingham Palace from the Memorial Gardens, which is made up of the Dominion Gates (Canada Gate, Australia Gate and South and West Africa Gates) and a vast central monument commemorating the death of Queen Victoria in 1901. (Shutterstock)

Buckingham Palace has served as the official London residence of the UK's sovereign since 1837. Today, it is the administrative headquarters of the Queen, where many official events and receptions are held. The State Rooms are open to the public every summer. It is also the London residence of the Prince Andrew and Prince Edward and the Countess of Wessex.

History
18TH CENTURY
King George III purchased Buckingham House in 1761 from Sir Charles Sheffield for the sum of £28,000 (about £6 million in modern money). George bought the house, which became known as the Queen's House, as a gift for his wife, Queen Charlotte, in order to provide a comfortable and well-located family home close to St James's Palace, where many court functions were held. It was here that 14 of George III's 15 children were born.

19TH CENTURY
The house passed to George IV on his accession in 1820, whereupon the King decided to undertake building work to convert it into a conveniently located pied-à-terre. The builders set to, but with works well underway

the King changed his mind and decided instead to transform it into a palace, with the help of his architect, John Nash.

Nash retained the main block of the Queen's House but doubled its size by adding a new suite of rooms – the State and Semi-State Rooms, which remain virtually

VITAL STATISTICS

LOCATION: *Westminster, London SW1*
OPENED: *1703*
MEASUREMENTS: *108m (355ft) wide across the front, 120m (394ft) deep (including the central quadrangle) and 24m (79ft) tall*
ROOMS: *775, including 19 State Rooms, 52 royal and guest bedrooms, 188 staff bedrooms, 92 offices and 78 bathrooms*
STAFF: *About 400, including domestic servants, chefs, footmen, cleaners, plumbers, gardeners, chauffeurs, electricians, and two people who look after the 300 clocks.*

unchanged since Nash's time – on the western, garden side. This was clad with Bath stone and styled to reflect the French neoclassical influence that the King favoured.

In order to fund the works, Parliament agreed to a budget of £150,000. The King, however, pressed for three times that amount as a more realistic figure. George was right: by 1829 the costs had skyrocketed, reaching nearly half a million pounds – an extravagance that cost Nash his job.

George IV never got to live in the palace, as he died the following year, whereupon his younger brother, William IV, acceded to the throne. William duly hired architect Edward Blore to complete the works but, like his brother, he never lived there either. So it was that Queen Victoria, King William's niece, became the first monarch to take up residence at the palace, in July 1837. The following year, in June 1838, she also became the first British sovereign to leave from Buckingham Palace for a coronation.

Victoria, however, quickly declared the palace to be unfit for her purposes, having no nurseries and insufficient guest bedrooms. She therefore called once more on the services of Blore, who removed the Marble Arch (relocating it to its current position in Hyde Park) and built a fourth wing, creating a quadrangle. He also added an attic floor to the main building, and further

Did you know?

When the Houses of Parliament were destroyed by fire in 1834, King William IV offered the palace as a new home for Parliament, but the offer was turned down.

external decorations in the form of marble friezes that had originally been intended for Marble Arch. All of this was completed by 1847, in time to accommodate Victoria and Albert's expanding family. It was partly funded by the sale of the Royal Pavilion in Brighton.

20TH CENTURY

Over the years, the soot and filthy air of Victorian London took its toll on the soft French stone that had been used to face the east wing, and in 1913 the decision was taken to reface the facade. The commission for a new design fell to Sir Aston Webb, a man who had previous experience with large buildings. Webb chose Portland stone, which stonemasons spent a year preparing before building work began. The refacing itself took a mere 13 weeks to complete.

US President George W. Bush and the Queen walk through the Queen's Gallery away from the press at Buckingham Palace during his state visit to the UK in November 2003 (PA Images)

Edward Griffiths, former Deputy Master of the Household stands in the White Drawing Room, designed by the architect John Nash, in the middle of preparations for the wedding reception of Prince William and Catherine Middleton, Buckingham Palace. (PA Images)

Other changes were taking place around the same time, too. These included the creation of the present forecourt of the palace as part of the Victoria Memorial scheme, and the installation of the extant gates and railings. All the work was completed just before the outbreak of World War I in 1914.

THE MODERN PALACE

Today, Buckingham Palace, one of the most famous landmarks in the UK, is a working building. It is often a focal point for significant national events, ranging from the Queen's jubilees to anniversaries of battles. These are marked by concerts, such as the one in 2002 that was staged in the garden to celebrate the Queen's Golden Jubilee and featured Brian May giving a memorable performance of *God Save The Queen* from the roof, as well as picnics to which members of the public are invited, fly-pasts and the announcements of births and deaths, which are attached to the palace railings. The palace is also the venue for investitures and events laid on in honour of visiting heads of state and other dignitaries. In all, it hosts almost 100,000 guests per year, as well as attracting some 15 million tourists.

The balcony

The balcony of Buckingham Palace is one of the most famous in the world, the backdrop to countless public appearances by royals and family photos that are reproduced all over the world. The first recorded such appearance took place in 1851, when Queen Victoria stepped on to the balcony during celebrations for the opening of the Great Exhibition. Since then, royal balcony appearances have marked many occasions, from the Queen's annual official birthday celebrations to the 75th anniversary of the Battle of Britain.

Refurbishments

Given the heavy foot traffic and age of the palace, it is perhaps little surprise that it has suffered some wear and tear. In 2016, a report summited by the Royal Trustees (the prime minister, the Chancellor of the Exchequer and the keeper of the privy purse) revealed that the palace's electrical cabling, plumbing and heating systems have not been updated since the 1950s and that the building's infrastructure is in urgent need of a complete overhaul to prevent long-term damage to the structure and its contents.

The Royal Trustees decided that the best way to replace these key services, and to ensure that the palace is fit for purpose for the next 50 years, is to undertake a phased schedule of works over 10 years. The programme's aim is to realise long-term financial and environmental benefits, as well as improvements to visitor access. The Queen gave assurances that the palace will remain occupied and fully operational for the duration of the reservicing.

The £369 million, decade-long reservicing programme was duly approved by Parliament and work started in April 2017. It is being funded through an increase in the Sovereign Grant.

PROPOSED WORKS

The refit programme will include:

· *renewing the palace's outdated boilers*
· *replacing 160km (100 miles) of vulcanised electrical cable*
· *restoring and renewing 32km (20 miles) of lead and cast-iron pipework*
· *increasing visitor access*
· *improving access and facilities for disabled visitors*
· *creating additional and better office space and meeting facilities*
· *improving energy efficiency*

WINDSOR CASTLE

With a history that stretches back some 1,000 years, Windsor Castle has been continuously occupied since its inception and remains the largest occupied castle in the world. Today, it is used by the Queen as a private home, often at the weekends and for more extended periods at other times of the year, and for formal duties, such as investitures and state visits, in its capacity as an official royal residence.

History

During its long and illustrious history, Windsor Castle has been home to successive monarchs. Many of these have made their mark by altering and refurbishing the buildings – whether for aesthetic or defensive purposes – all of which have helped to produce the iconic castle that stands today.

11TH CENTURY

William the Conqueror chose the position for the original motte-and-bailey castle, high above the River Thames and just a day's march from the Tower of London, where it was intended to guard the western approaches to the capital. Although that original wooden structure is long gone, the outer walls of the current castle are in the same position as those of that first incarnation, as is the central mound supporting the Round Tower and the Upper Ward.

VITAL STATISTICS

LOCATION: *Windsor, Berkshire*
OPENED: *1070*
MEASUREMENTS: *The floor area of the castle is approximately 45,000sq m (485,000sq ft) and occupies 12 acres of land*
ROOMS: *1,000*
STAFF: *The castle is home to 150 people and the monarch has approximately 430 full-time and part-time staff (the number of staff fluctuates, depending on whether or not the Queen is in residence)*

12TH–14TH CENTURIES

In the 1170s, Henry II rebuilt in stone the Round Tower, the outer walls of the Upper Ward and most of the Lower Ward, and the Royal Apartments in the Upper Ward. These fortifications paid off and the castle withstood a lengthy siege during the 1st Barons War at the start of the 13th century. Later in that century, Henry III undertook building works to create a luxurious palace within the castle walls, which his successor, Edward III, then demolished and rebuilt in an even more extravagant style. Called St George's Hall and intended for the use of the Knights of his new Order of the Garter, this structure stood for some 200 years, up to and through the Tudor period.

A view of Windsor Castle's East Terrace and Royal Apartments. (Shutterstock)

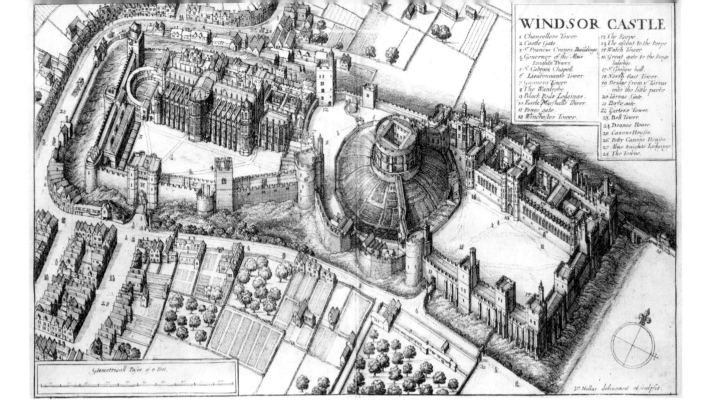

An etching of Windsor Castle, England, by Bohemian artist Wenceslaus Hollar, dating from the 1600s. (Alamy)

15TH–16TH CENTURIES

Monarchs continued to use Windsor Castle as both a residence and for royal entertaining throughout this period, and increasingly so in the latter half of the 15th century and into the 16th century. Among the notable events held there were the visit by the Holy Roman Emperor in 1417, lavish feasts in honour of the Order of the Garter – particularly the one held by Henry VII in 1488 – and visits by foreign kings and dignitaries, especially from the end of the 15th century.

Successive kings made many alterations, including the construction by Edward IV of the present-day St George's Chapel in 1475, a three-storied tower built by Henry VII at the end of the 15th century, and Henry VIII's long terrace along the outside wall of the Upper Ward and the rebuilt principle gateway. Later Tudor monarchs made other smaller changes, alongside running repairs and refits of existing structures.

At intervals throughout the 16th century, the castle was used as a haven, from plague as well as political threats, and Elizabeth I spent much of her time there, entertaining and using the premises for diplomatic engagements, although lack of space, or a lack of it, continued to be an issue.

17TH CENTURY

This problem vexed James I, too, as he liked to use the castle primarily for hunting and socialising with his friends, whom he struggled at times to accommodate in individual rooms. Charles I was altogether more of an aesthete and in 1629 had the castle extensively surveyed by a team that included Inigo Jones, although in the end little work was actually carried out.

When Civil War broke out, the castle was captured by the Parliamentarian Colonel John Venn in 1642 and went on to become both the headquarters for various Parliamentarian commanders, including Oliver Cromwell, and a prison for, among others, Charles I himself, before he was moved to Hampton Court. After Charles's execution, his body was brought back for burial, without ceremony, in St George's Chapel. During this period, looting became rife and many objects were either stolen or destroyed, deer were killed and fences were broken up and used as firewood. What's more, squatters took up residence, wreaking further havoc on the buildings and their contents.

The extent of the damage became apparent once the monarchy had been restored in 1660, and this, along with a change in taste for what constituted a 'successful' palace, led Charles II to make major changes in order to modernise the castle and refashion it in his preferred Baroque style. To tackle the task, Charles II appointed Prince Rupert, who reworked the defences, repaired the Round Tower and reconstructed the tennis court that had been installed by Henry VIII. Charles also hired architect Hugh May, who expanded out into the North Terrace in order to provide the enfiladed rooms required by French court etiquette, and sympathetically rebuilt the medieval hall and chapel built by Edward III. He also created a new set of State Apartments in the 1670s and laid out the 5km (3 mile) Long Walk leading due south from the castle into Windsor Great Park.

THE WINDSOR FIRE, 1992

In November 1992 a spotlight in the Private Chapel of Windsor Castle came into contact with a curtain and ignited the material, starting a devastating fire that seriously damaged or destroyed nine major rooms and around 100 other rooms, covering an area of 9,000sq m (96,875sq ft) – about one-fifth of the castle. In all, it took 15 hours and 1.5 million gallons of water to extinguish the blaze, and five years to restore the castle, at a cost of £37 million. Around 70 per cent of the money was raised from opening Buckingham Palace's State Rooms to visitors over a two-month period, and the rest came from savings in the annual grant-in-aid fund.

18TH CENTURY

Early monarchs of the 18th century had little use for Windsor Castle, preferring other royal residences such as Hampton Court, St James's Palace and Kensington Palace. Rooms and apartments were therefore loaned to friends of the Crown and prominent widows, and by around 1740 the castle had become a tourist attraction rather than a functioning residence.

In the 1760s, however, George III became the king and, disliking Hampton Court, moved into Windsor, implementing extensive renovations. Latterly favouring the Gothic style, he and architect James Wyatt attempted to restyle the exterior of the Upper Ward with Gothic features, such as new battlement and turrets, and a Gothic staircase, as well as creating several new rooms and installing many works of art, often taken from other royal residences. He also undertook extensive work in the Great Park. It was here, in the State Apartments, that George was confined towards the end of his life.

19TH CENTURY

George III's son, George IV, was also a lover of fine decoration and as Prince Regent he expanded the Great Lodge in Windsor Great Park. On acceding to the throne in 1820, he instigated a number of alterations with the help of architect, Sir Jeffry Wyatville, the intention being that royal palaces should reflect the king's wealth and increasing influence on the global stage.

The buildings were refashioned in a mixture of styles – the king preferred Rococo while Wyatville favoured the Gothic – with many areas being remodelled, new towers being added, the Round Tower being raised to greater prominence and various other areas being rebuilt or restructured. One of the most impressive additions was the Waterloo Chamber, created to display portraits by Sir Thomas Lawrence that had been commissioned to commemorate the defeat of Napoleon at the battle of Waterloo in 1815.

All of this came at a very high price: £1 million, which equates to about £820 million now. George died before it was completed, but much of the work had been done by the time Wyatville died in 1840.

Despite purportedly complaining early on in her reign that she found the castle 'dull and tiresome', Queen Victoria, along with her husband Prince Albert, made Windsor Castle their primary royal residence when she became queen in 1837. It was here that many state and

In the restored St George's Hall, devastated in the fire of 1992, the tables are laid for a state banquet held in honour of the Indian president Prathibha Patil, in Windsor Castle. October 2009. (PA Images)

Thousands of daffodils are arranged on the Grand Staircase of Windsor Castle, in preparation for the wedding of Prince Charles and Camilla. (PA Images)

social events were held, with visitors coming from far afield, aided in no small part by the growth of the railway and advances in steamships. Victoria was very involved in the detailed planning of such visits, which were rigid in their formality. It was also here that Albert died of typhoid in 1861, and he was buried in a mausoleum that Queen Victoria constructed at Frogmore House in Windsor Home Park. For a long time afterwards the castle was kept in a state of mourning, with the Queen living there when on official business.

Victoria implemented some changes during her long reign, none of which made the castle, which was renowned for being cold and draughty, especially comfortable. She also eschewed gas lighting, and by the end of her life there was only limited electric lighting.

20TH CENTURY–PRESENT

When he succeeded to the throne in 1901, Edward VII set about rigorously updating the castle, including installing electric lighting, central heating, telephone wires, and garages to house the new motorcars. George V continued his work, with Queen Mary seeking out and buying furniture that had previously been lost or sold. He also employed a large staff. Such was the castle's importance by this time that when the king sought a new family name to replace the Germanic one during World War I, he chose Windsor.

Despite the improved comfort, Edward VIII did not live at the castle during his short reign before he abdicated. His brother, George VI, initially favoured the Royal Lodge, though he and his wife, Elizabeth, did subsequently move into the castle, which was home to the young princesses Elizabeth and Margaret while they remained

The royal kitchens at Windsor Castle as preparations are underway for the reception banquet after the wedding of Prince Harry and Meghan Markle. These the oldest functioning kitchens in the world, and have been in constant use for 750 years. (PA Images)

in London. When she became queen, Elizabeth made the castle her primary weekend residence, something that remains the case to this day.

Official uses

In addition to spending many weekends at Windsor Castle, the Queen takes up official residence for a month over the Easter period (March–April). Called 'Easter Court', this period is notable for the occasional 'dine and sleep' events the Queen hosts for guests, which may include politicians and public figures. In June, the Queen returns for a week, when she attends the service of the Order of the Garter and the Royal Ascot race meeting. Numerous banquets and state events are also held at the castle throughout the year, for family occasions, such as weddings, baptisms and funerals.

St George's Chapel

This chapel is an active place of worship, with daily services open to the public. The chapel has been the location of numerous royal weddings, including those of Prince Edward and Sophie Rhys-Jones in June 1999, Prince Harry and Meghan Markle in 2018, and Princess Eugenie and Jack Brooksbank, also in 2018.

Open to the public

Windsor Castle is a busy visitor attraction. Many parts are open to the public year round, including the precincts, the State Apartments, Queen Mary's famous dolls' house, St George's Chapel and the Albert Memorial Chapel. Changing the Guard takes place regularly. When the Queen is in official residence, the parade provides a colourful spectacle in the quadrangle.

PALACE OF HOLYROODHOUSE

VITAL STATISTICS

LOCATION: *Edinburgh, Scotland*
OPENED: *1671–78*
MEASUREMENTS: *Built on a quadrangle layout, about 70m (230ft) square*
ROOMS: *289*
STAFF: *106*

T he official residence of the Queen in Scotland, the Palace of Holyroodhouse – commonly known as Holyrood Palace – has been used by kings and queens of the Scots for centuries and continues to function in an official capacity today. The Queen stays there for a week during the summer, when she carries out various ceremonies and engagements, such as investitures. The rest of the time, parts of the palace are open to the public, while the State Apartments are used for official dining and state entertaining.

History
16TH AND 17TH CENTURIES
The earliest surviving part of the existing palace, the north-west tower, was built as part of a Gothic palace next door to the Augustinian Holyrood Abbey in 1528 for James V. Mary Queen of Scots lived in the royal apartments in the north-west tower from 1561 to 1567, married both of her husbands and gave birth to her son, James VI of Scotland, there. James took up residence in the palace at the end of the 16th century, aged 13, but when he became king of England in 1603, he moved to London and the palace ceased to be the seat of the permanent court. During the Civil War, part of the palace was set on fire while occupied by Cromwell's troops.

In 1660, the Restoration saw Charles II take the throne, and repairs were immediately made so that the Privy Council could once more convene at Holyrood. During the 1670s, plans for the complete reconstruction of the palace were implemented and the current three-storey building was constructed.

18TH CENTURY
Following the union of Scotland and England in 1707, Holyroodhouse no longer maintained its principle functions. However, it continued to provide grace-and-favour accommodation for nobles, primarily in the Queen's Apartments, and it was still used for the election of representative peers. The King's Apartments, however, lay neglected and disused throughout the century, and other parts of the palace suffered, too.

19TH CENTURY
At the turn of the century, following the French Revolution, the youngest brother of Louis XVI – the Comte d'Artois – was permitted to live at the Palace of Holyroodhouse. His stay, from 1796 to 1803, saw the King's Apartments being renovated.

When George IV visited the Palace of Holyroodhouse in 1822 he ordered repairs to be made over the next 10 years. Queen Victoria made more personal use of the palace, having ordered renovations to be made and some of the sitting nobles who inhabited the grace-and-favour rooms to be moved out. This having been done, Victoria took up a second-floor apartment in 1871, converting the former royal apartment into dining and drawing rooms and creating a throne room. The historic apartments in the 16th-century north-west tower were opened to public from 1854. The palace was formally designated as the monarch's official residence in Scotland in the 1920s and is used still as the venue for various state engagements.

The Palace of Hollyroodhouse, Edinburgh. (Shutterstock)

ST JAMES'S PALACE

VITAL STATISTICS

LOCATION: *St James's, London*

OPENED: *1536*

MEASUREMENTS: *Many buildings comprise the palace complex, so it's hard to say*

Rooms: Many buildings comprise the palace complex, so it's hard to say

STAFF: *The number varies*

Standing on the site of a former leper hospital, from which it derives its name, St James's Palace has had a long and illustrious history since it was built by Henry VIII. Today, although it is no longer home to a monarch, it is the senior royal palace in the UK, the official residence of the sovereign and the official base of the Royal Court.

History

16TH AND 17TH CENTURIES

On the orders of Henry VIII the palace was built in the Tudor style, and construction lasted from 1531 to 1536. The king's intention was that the palace would act as a smaller, secondary residence to Whitehall, where the king could find respite from formal court life. Built around a number of courtyards, the palace was constructed from red brick with darker red-brick detailing, and featured a striking four-storey gatehouse with crenellated octagonal towers and decorated with the initials 'HA', for Henry and Anne (Boleyn).

A few years later, in 1544, parts of the palace were remodelled and Hans Holbein was commissioned to paint the ceilings. It was in this 'pleasant royal house' that two of Henry's children – Henry Fitzroy and Mary I – died, and where another of his children, Elizabeth, spent some of her childhood. It was also here in 1588 that Elizabeth, now queen and living in the palace, planned the attack on the Spanish Armada and is said to have prepared her famous address to her troops assembled

> **Did you know?**
> St James's Palace is the oldest royal palace in the UK.

at Tilbury. The future Charles II and James II were both born and christened there, as were Mary of York (Mary II), Anne of York (Queen Anne) and James Francis Edward Stuart (the Old Pretender).

During the Interregnum years (1649–1660), Oliver Cromwell turned the palace into barracks, but it was restored when Charles II took the throne; he constructed neighbouring St James's Park during the same period.

18TH CENTURY

After the Palace of Whitehall was destroyed by fire in 1698, St James's Palace became the primary residence and administrative centre of every monarch until William IV. By the end of the century, however, the king of the day, George III, was finding the premises too cramped for his growing family, so he bought

The Capella Musicale Pontificia (CMP), the Pope's Choir, also known as the Sistine Chapel Choir, sing with the Choir of Her Majesty's Chapel Royal, at the Chapel Royal, St James's Palace in London. (PA Images)

The Queen arrives at a reception to mark the 60th anniversary of Cruse Bereavement Care at St James's Palace in London. (PA Images)

Buckingham House, which became the family home, with St James's only used for formal state occasions. Accordingly, when refurbishments were made, work was only carried out in the State Apartments and not the living quarters.

19TH CENTURY AND 20TH CENTURY

A few years later, in 1809, the palace was partly destroyed by fire. Affected areas included the monarch's private apartments, which were never restored, unlike the State Rooms, which were restored by 1813. These continued to be used for court levées – formal receptions at which officials, diplomats and military officers of the armed services were presented individually to the sovereign – until 1939. The royal family, however, from Queen Victoria onwards, no longer used the palace as their primary residence, although Victoria and other royals were married in the Chapel Royal there.

THE PALACE TODAY

St James's Palace is the ceremonial meeting place of the Accession Council and includes the Court of James, where all new monarchs are proclaimed. It is used to host official receptions for visiting heads of state and charities of which royal family members are patrons. In addition, it contains offices used by Prince Charles's team and other organisations associated with the royal family, such as The Royal Collection Trust. The palace is also the London residence of Princess Beatrice of York and the Queen's cousin, Princess Alexandra.

It is also the location of the Chapel Royal, where many royal christenings have taken place through the years. It was here that Prince George in 2011 and Meghan Markle in 2018 were baptised into the Church of England.

> ### *Did you know?*
> In the state apartments there is a fireplace dating from Henry VIII's reign with the initials 'HA' for Henry and Anne Boleyn (his second of six wives) on one side and just 'H' on the other because by the time it was finished Anne had been found guilty of treason and was beheaded on 19 May 1536.

KENSINGTON PALACE

Kensington Palace, or 'KP' as it is known, is a working royal residence that contains the offices and London residences of Prince William and the and Duchess of Cambridge, as well as those of the Duke and Duchess of Gloucester, the Duke and Duchess of Kent and Prince and Princess Michael of Kent. It is also home to many paintings and objects from the Royal Collection, and is the preferred venue at which national successes are celebrated. The State Rooms are open to the public, attracting thousands of visitors every year.

VITAL STATISTICS

LOCATION: *Kensington and Chelsea, London*
OPENED: *1605*
MEASUREMENTS: *Several apartments in 350 acres*
ROOMS: *The palace comprises many apartments with varying numbers or rooms. Apartment 1A – the home of the Duke and Duchess of Cambridge – has 20 stately rooms*

History

17TH AND 18TH CENTURIES

The original two-storey Jacobean mansion was built in 1605 by Sir George Coppin, and was bought by Heneage Finch, 1st Earl of Nottingham in 1619. In 1689, William III and Mary bought the mansion, known as Nottingham House, for £20,000 from his secretary of state, the Earl of Nottingham, the location of the house being better suited to the health needs of the asthmatic king than that of Whitehall Palace.

Christopher Wren was then commissioned to extend and improve the existing house by adding three-storey pavilions to each of the mansion's four corners and reorienting the house to face west. He also built north and south wings to flank the approach, and the property was surrounded with lawns and formal stately gardens. This work was completed in 1689, when the royal court took up residence, and remained there for the next 70 years, until the death of George II in 1760.

During this period, the palace was the favoured residence of successive sovereigns, many of whom made additional changes to the house and surrounds.

A view of Kensington Palace in London, with the statue of King William III in the foreground, April 2017. (Shutterstock)

These included the Queen's Gallery, commissioned by Mary, and the Queen's Apartments devised by Christopher Wren upon Queen Anne's orders, as part of the completion of the renovations started by William and Mary. Queen Anne also made extensive changes to the gardens, including the intricately decorated Orangery, which was modified by John Vanbrugh.

After Anne's death in 1714, George I created three new State Rooms, which were decorated in extravagant style by William Kent, and went on to ask Kent to decorate many other areas in similar fashion. His successor, George II, was less interested in such details, however, and left the running of the palace to Queen Caroline. When she died, many rooms were neglected and fell into disrepair. By the time he died and George III took the throne in 1760, the palace was only used for minor royalty. These included the sixth son of George III, Prince Augustus Frederick, who took apartments in the south-west corner that came to be known as Apartment 1. Here, Augustus, who went on to be elected president of the Royal Society, collected thousands of books, many

clocks, and a wide range of singing birds that were free to fly around the rooms.

19TH CENTURY

Queen Victoria, King William IV's niece, was born, christened and brought up in the palace and it was there that she received news of her accession in 1837 from the Lord Chamberlain and the Archbishop of Canterbury. Nevertheless, Victoria immediately moved into Buckingham Palace and reigned from there rather than St James's or Kensington, as had been expected. She never again stayed at Kensington Palace, granting rooms to family members, including the Duke and Duchess of Teck, the future Queen Mary's parents; Mary was born there in 1867. Various other members of the royal family also inhabited apartments within the palace, as they do today.

20TH CENTURY–PRESENT

In addition to its numerous royal inhabitants, during World War I George V allowed some of the rooms to be used by people working for Irish POWs and Irish soldiers at the front. All of the inhabitants, whether royal or not, had to adhere to the same rationing as the rest of the nation.

In World War II, the palace was hit by an incendiary bomb, which damaged many of the buildings, especially the Queen's Apartments. Elsewhere, Apartment 34 became the Headquarters of Personnel Section. The gardens were filled with sandbags, trenches and anti-aircraft guns.

After the war, repairs were not made for a few years and the palace suffered some neglect. Nevertheless, Prince Philip stayed at Kensington in his grandmother's apartment in 1947 during the period between his engagement and his marriage to Elizabeth, along with many other royal relatives in the various apartments. For example, Princess Margaret lived there, as did Diana, Princess of Wales, both when she was still married to Charles, and after the couple divorced.

Apartment 1A

Prince William and the Duchess of Cambridge and their family live at the 20-room apartment 1A, formerly the home of Princess Margaret. This was extensively renovated over the course of 18 months from 2011. Work included major roof repairs and asbestos removal, and cost the taxpayer £4.5 million, as revealed in the 2014 Sovereign Grant Report. Prince William and the Duchess paid privately for a second family kitchen to supplement the 'working kitchen' that is used for official events.

The Prince and Princess of Wales with their son Prince William during a photo session in the sitting room at Kensington Palace, Christmas 1982. (PA Images)

BALMORAL CASTLE AND ESTATE

Balmoral is one of two personal and private residences that the monarch personally owns. Estimated to be worth £155 million today, it is where the Queen and her family enjoy private summer holidays. Elizabeth's granddaughter, Princess Eugenie, said it is where the Queen is 'the most happy' and where she occupies her time, when not working on her government red boxes, with 'walks, picnics and a lot of dogs.' The Queen is so strict about maintaining her family's privacy at Balmoral that she rarely lets photographers into her summer home. She did, however, allow the Duchess of Cambridge to take some photos on her first visit there. The castle is classified by Historic Scotland as a category A listed building, and costs around £3 million annually to run.

History
19TH CENTURY

Queen Victoria and Prince Albert purchased the estate and original castle outright in 1852 for £31,000, but, finding the previous property too small, decided to construct a new building. They commissioned architect William Smith to draw up plans, although Albert, who took a great interest in the project, also had a hand in the design.

Queen Victoria laid the foundation stone for the newly built castle on 28 September 1853. It was completed by 1856, in the Scottish Baronial style. Albert also set about landscaping the area, starting a programme of improvements that lasted for several years. Victoria spent more of her time at the castle than anywhere else.

20TH CENTURY–PRESENT

When Victoria died in 1901, Balmoral passed to her son and heir Edward VII, who did not make much use of it, only staying there for three to four weeks a year. George V inherited it from his father and, like his grandmother, loved visiting it, as did his son George VI. The Queen holidays at the castle in the summer, where she is joined by other members of the royal family.

The main entrance of Balmoral Castle. (Shutterstock)

SANDRINGHAM HOUSE AND ESTATE

VITAL STATISTICS

LOCATION: *Sandringham, Norfolk*

OPENED: *1870*

MEASUREMENTS: *20,000-acre estate valued at an estimated £52 million. The gardens and the country park comrise 600 acres of the estate with the gardens extending to 49 acres Rooms: The house has been added to extensively and the current number of rooms is not known*

STAFF: *Numbers increase when the Queen is in residence to around 430, both full and part time*

Sandringham House is a country house near the village of Sandringham in Norfolk, England. (Shutterstock)

The Queen inherited Sandringham from her father in 1952. It is one of two personal and private residences owned by the monarch. The Queen usually celebrates Christmas there, where she is joined by many members of the royal family.

History

19TH CENTURY

The original Sandringham House and its 8,000 hectare estate was bought in 1862 for the 21-year-old Prince of Wales, the future Edward VII, as a country residence to which he could retreat from London life. After his marriage to Princess Alexandra of Denmark in 1863, the prince moved into the Georgian house, but as their family grew and they had to entertain more frequently, more space was required. Edward therefore commissioned A.J. Humbert to build a new property on the site, in place of the existing building. Designed in the Jacobean style and completed in 1870, it had brick walls, stone dressings and gabled roofs. The only part of the old house to survive was the conservatory, which was converted into a billiard room. Later additions included a ballroom and another conservatory.

Disaster struck in 1851, when fire broke out and destroyed 14 bedrooms on the upper storeys, and damaged many lower ones. Repairs were undertaken and a new suite of bedrooms was added.

20TH CENTURY

After the death of Edward VII in 1910, the house passed to his son, George V, who loved the place and continued to use it as a retreat from court life. He famously wrote, 'Dear old Sandringham, the place I love better than anywhere else in the world.' In time, it passed to George VI, the Queen's father, who also loved the house and estate. Both kings died there. The Queen, too, enjoys spending time there, as does Prince Philip, who took overall responsibility for the management of the estate when it passed to the Queen, and who has retired there.

Currently, the estate employs more than 200 people, ranging from farmers and foresters to gamekeepers and gardeners. More than half of the estate is let to tenant farmers; the rest is farmed in hand or used for forestry (the estate has its own sawmill). There are also two studs, a fruit farm and a 600-acre country park.

Sandringham gardens

Over time, the gardens at Sandringham have been extensively altered. In 1908, the gardens were opened to the public by Edward VII, and a summerhouse was built for Queen Alexandra in 1912. During the reign of George VI many further changes were made, including the elaborate borders and parterres being dug up during World War II and replaced by less labour-intensive lawns. The North Garden was also created around the same time. In the 1960s.

The royal stud

The stud was established at Sandringham in 1886 by the then Prince of Wales. It quickly became very successful and highly influential in the development of the national thoroughbred bloodstock. The mare Perdita II, for example, produced two of racing's legends: Persimmon, which won the St Leger and the Derby in 1896; and Diamond Jubilee, which won the 1900 Triple Crown. The Prince of Wales ploughed the prize money from his winning horses into Sandringham, particularly the vast Walled Kitchen Gardens. Today, the Queen takes a particular interest in bloodstock breeding and has been rewarded by considerable success on the racecourse.

Wood Farm, Sandringham

Prince Philip downsized following his retirement in 2017 and now spends much of his time living in a spacious cottage on the Sandringham Estate. He spends his time reading and painting, and entertaining friends.

Acquired by Albert Edward, Prince of Wales (later Edward VII), the former farm manager's cottage lies in a secluded part of the estate. It was used by George V's son, Prince John, who suffered from epilepsy, from 1917 until his death in 1919. Between then and now, it has been used by various members of the royal family, including divorced spouses of royals so that they could be close to their children, especially at Christmas.

Anmer Hall

Anmer Hall, the Grade II listed country home of the Prince William and the Duchess of Cambridge, is located on the Sandringham Estate. It was given to William and Kate by the Queen following their wedding in 2011.

The 10-bedroom Georgian manor dates from the 18th century, though building on the site dates to much earlier. It originally belonged to the Coldham family, from at least 1705. The Prince of Wales, later Edward VII bought Anmer Hall in 1896. After that it was leased to 1st Baron Rugby and later his daughter, Penelope. Next, it was leased to the Queen's first cousin the Duke of Kent. From 1990 to 2000 it was rented by the van Cutsem family, friends of the Prince of Wales, and Prince William spent time there as a child as a guest. In 2012, the Queen allocated the property to Prince William, who lived there with Kate full time following Princess Charlotte's birth in 2015, while William was still working with the East Anglian Air Ambulance. The couple now uses Anmer Hall as their country property, with their main residence being Apartment 1A, Kensington Palace.

The hall, which has undergone renovation, now includes a swimming pool, a private tennis court and 10 bedrooms. It's also has a no-fly zone in place above it, which means the family is able to relax in peace.

THE QUEEN'S TOP FIVE RACEHORSES

1. DUNFERMLINE *(foaled in 1974) was a double Classic-winning filly that romped home first at the Epsom Oaks and St. Leger in the same 1977 season, the Queen's Silver Jubilee year.*

2. ESTIMATE *(foaled in 2009) was an 80th birthday gift to the Queen from the Aga Khan, and is one of the Queen's best ever racehorses. In 2013, she won the Gold Cup at Royal Ascot.*

3. PALL MALL *(foaled in 1955) was the Queen's first British 2000 Guineas-winning colt, which also won the 1958 and 1959 Lockinge Stakes at Newbury.*

4. HIGHCLERE *(foaled in 1971) was a top-class filly and brood mare. In 1974, she won the 1000 Guineas at Newmarket and France's Prix de Diane. Her daughter, Height of Fashion, would go on to produce 2000 Guineas and Epsom Derby champion*

Nashwan and multiple Group race winners Nayef and Unfuwain.

5. CARROZZA *(foaled in 1954) was the Queen's first British Classic winner. Trained at Warren Place Stables, the three-year-old was the 1957 champion of the Epsom Oaks – a success that helped the Queen finish the 1957 season as Champion Owner.*

CLARENCE HOUSE

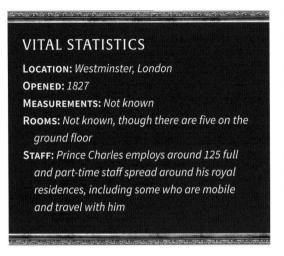

VITAL STATISTICS

LOCATION: *Westminster, London*
OPENED: *1827*
MEASUREMENTS: *Not known*
ROOMS: *Not known, though there are five on the ground floor*
STAFF: *Prince Charles employs around 125 full and part-time staff spread around his royal residences, including some who are mobile and travel with him*

The Prince of Wales' Standard is raised over Clarence House for the first time in August 2003 as Prince Charles takes up official residence. The banner includes the Royal Arms, the Coronet of the Heir Apparent and the Arms of the Principality of Wales. (PA Images)

Clarence House is the official London residence of the Prince of Wales and the Duchess of Cornwall. The four-storey house is also the location of the offices of Prince Charles's Household, the team that works behind the scenes to liaise with the many organisations Charles is involved with. The main rooms are used for official entertaining and for audiences with the prince.

Clarence House is also now open to the public for two months during the summer. Visitors are given a guided tour of the five rooms and adjoining spaces on the ground floor.

History
19TH CENTURY

The John Nash-designed house was built between 1825 and 1827 for Prince William Henry, Duke of Clarence – from whom the house took its name. Having acceded the throne in 1830, King William IV chose to live there, rather than in adjacent St James's Palace, which he found cramped. Next, the property passed to William's sister, Princess Augusta Sophia, and after she died, to Queen Victoria's mother, Princess Victoria of Saxe-Coburg-Saalfeld. It then became the home of Victoria's second son, Prince Alfred, Duke of Edinburgh, until he died in 1900.

20TH CENTURY – PRESENT

In 1900, Prince Alfred's younger brother, Arthur, Duke of Connaught, made Clarence House his residence until he died in 1942. During this period the library of the School of Oriental and African studies was housed there, until World War II broke out and the collection was relocated. The house suffered some damage during the Blitz, and after Arthur's death in 1942 it was used as the headquarters of the Red Cross and the St John Ambulance Brigade for the remainder of the war.

Following the marriage of Princess Elizabeth and Philip in 1947 the house became the princess's London residence and Prince Philip directed a major renovation programme. It was here that Princess Anne was born. After George VI's death in 1952, the Queen and her family moved to Buckingham Palace and in 1953 Queen Elizabeth, the Queen Mother moved into Clarence House along with Princess Margaret. Margaret lived there until she moved to her apartment in Kensington Palace. The Queen Mother lived there until her death in 2002, whereupon Clarence House was left to Charles.

The house underwent extensive refurbishment and redecoration before Charles moved in a year later, relocating from the relatively small York House at St James's Palace. Asbestos was taken out, plumbing was updated, the house was completely rewired, colour schemes were adjusted in most rooms, new textiles were introduced, and several new pieces from the Royal Collection and from Prince Charles's own art collection were added. The works – which were overseen by interior designer Robert Kime – cost the taxpayer £4.5 million, from a grant-in-aid set aside for palace maintenance. The prince used £1.6 million of his own money for any extras.

HIGHGROVE HOUSE AND ESTATE

Highgrove is the family home of Prince Charles and the Duchess of Cornwall, as well as being the venue for many briefings and receptions. The Georgian house, garden and nearby farmland, Duchy Home Farm, is owned by the Duchy of Cornwall, which bought the estate in 1980. The house is ideally situated in Gloucestershire, with easy access to London, Wales and various other parts of Britain, including the western counties that are home to many of the Duchy's other properties.

History

19TH CENTURY

Highgrove House was built between in 1796 to 1798 by local squire John Paul, and is believed to have been designed by architect Anthony Keck. From then until 1860 the property belonged to John Paul's descendants, when the house was sold. It was sold again in 1864 to a barrister, William Yatman, who rebuilt the medieval spire of Tetbury church and rehung the bells. He quit Highgrove, however, after a fire in 1893 that destroyed the interior of much of the house. The house was subsequently rebuilt at a cost of £6,000 by new owner, Arthur Mitchell.

20TH CENTURY–PRESENT

Mitchell's family sold Highgrove at the end of World War II to Lt Col Gwyn Morgan, who in 1956 sold it to the Macmillan family for £89,000. The family lived there until 1980, when the son of former Prime Minister Harold Macmillan sold it for £730,000. Then, later that year, in August 1980, the Highgrove Estate was purchased by the Duchy of Cornwall for an undisclosed figure understood to be between £800,000 and £1,000,000. Having been appointed tenant for life by the Duchy, Charles remodelled the Georgian house with neo-classical additions, as well as carrying out essential repairs.

Highgrove House in 1980, just after it was bought by the Duchy of Cornwall. The 10-bedroom Georgian mansion has been extensively renovated since. PA Images)

Prince Charles meets the President of Rwanda, Paul Kagame, at Highgrove in July 2019. (PA Images)

Did you know?
All profits made by Highgrove from the sale of garden tours, events and products are donated to the Prince of Wales's Charitable Foundation.

A swimming pool was also installed – a wedding present to Prince Charles and Diana by the British Army – and extra land was purchased in the form of Broadfield Farm, a 420-acre farm on the opposite side of Tetbury, and other holdings. Beehive pavilions and a beef yard were among the buildings Charles commissioned, and cottages on the estate were renovated.

The house itself was given Grade II listed status in March 1985, as were the Coach House, the Lodge and Gate Piers to the east. Today, the extensive gardens – which include a walled kitchen garden, a wild garden and a formal garden – attract more than 30,000 visitors a year, who come for guided tours on selected dates between February and October.

Environmentally friendly features

In line with Charles's view on ethical and environmental concerns, Highgrove House and the estate are run along eco-friendly lines. Features include a reed bed sewage system, which also provides a habitat for dragonflies,

and the planting of rare trees, plants and heritage seeds to ensure these varieties continue to flourish into the future. In the house itself, energy-saving bulbs and solar lights are used where appropriate, and there is a comprehensive composting system. Biomass boilers and ground and air source heat pumps provide heating and hot water.

Duchy Home Farm

In 1985, Charles decided to make the 900-acre Duchy Home Farm a completely organic farming system. Managed by David Wilson, it is today a flagship for organic farming. There are around 100 sheep of mixed breeds, including Lleyn, Cotswold and Shropshire, as well as a dairy herd consisting of 200 milkers and a beef herd that comprises about 100 cattle made up of Aberdeen Angus, Gloucester and British Whites. The farm shop sells milk, grain, pork, barley, fruit and vegetables and the farm also supplies restaurants, supermarkets and nearby schools.

A view of the gardens and rear of Highgrove at the launch for the Coronation Meadows Initiative by Prince Charles in June 2013. (PA Images)

OTHER RESIDENCES

Craigowan Lodge, Scotland

Situated about 1.6km (1 mile) from the main house at Balmoral, this seven-bedroom stone house was often used as a home by Charles and Diana when they were at the estate, and today is a guest house for VIP visitors. In the past, too, it provided sanctuary for Michael Andreevich Romanoff, a member of the Russian imperial family, who spent most of World War II there.

Birkhall, Scotland

Birkhall is the private residence of the Prince Charles and the Duchess of Cornwall in Scotland and the former home of Queen Elizabeth, The Queen Mother. It is a 53,000-acre estate on Royal Deeside, Aberdeenshire, to the south-west of Ballater. Charles and Camilla spend their summer break here each year.

Dumfries House, Scotland

Set in 2,000 acres of land in Ayrshire, 18th-century Dumfries House is considered by many to be one of Britain's most beautiful stately homes. Saved by the intervention of Charles (Duke of Rothesay in Scotland) in 2007, it is now open year round to the public.

Llwynywermod, Wales

Situated near Llandovery in Carmarthenshire, this is Charles and Camilla's private Welsh home. Bought in 2007 by the Duchy of Cornwall, the farmhouse was refurbished using local materials and skills.

Tamarisk House, Isles of Scilly

The Isles of Scilly and around one-third of the residential buildings across the five islands are owned by the Duchy of Cornwall Estate. Charles's private residence, Tamarisk House, is located on the main island of St Mary's.

Nottingham Cottage and Ivy Cottage,

A grace-and-favour cottage in the grounds of Kensington palace, nicknamed 'Nott Cott', Nottingham Cottage was designed by Christopher Wren and named after Nottingham House, as Kensington Palace was known when it was first bought by the royal family. It has been well used over the years, by members of the royal family as well as their staff. In recent times, Prince William and Catherine, and then Prince Harry lived at Nottingham Cottage, and it was there that Harry proposed to Meghan Markle. Nearby is Ivy Cottage, another grace-and-favour property used for staff until Princess Eugenie,

younger daughter of Prince Andrew, moved in with her husband Jack Brooksbank after their 2018 wedding.

Frogmore Cottage, Windsor Castle

A Grade II listed Crown Estate house that dates to 1801, Frogmore Cottage is now the UK home of Harry and Meghan, who undertook considerable restructuring, at a cost of £2.4 million, to convert it from a five-apartment property to a single home. Controversially, the cost of this was initially covered by the Sovereign Grant. In January 2020, as part of stepping back from their royal duties, and becoming financially independent, the couple announced they would be paying back this sum. They had paid for fixtures and fittings privately.

Royal Lodge, Windsor Castle

Royal Lodge is a Grade II listed building that was built in 1946. Prince Andrew now lives there, as does his ex-wife Sarah, Duchess of York, in a separate part of the house.

Prince Charles, known as the Duke of Rothesay when in Scotland, at a ceremony to present service medals to soldiers from the 51st Highland, 7th Battalion, The Royal Regiment of Scotland in the grounds of Birkhall in Ballater, Aberdeenshire, October 2012. (PA Images)

A GUESTHOUSE IN DRACULA COUNTRY

Having been struck by the beauty and rich heritage of Romania during his first visit in 1988, Prince Charles later bought and carefully renovated a traditional farm, Zalanpatak, which lies in an almost inaccessible area deep in the heart of the country. It is composed of several buildings, a patch of forest, extensive flower meadows and various mineral springs and small brooks. The property is also characterised by its rich biodiversity of plants, mushrooms, insects, birds and large mammals including bears (sometimes crossing the back yard). Members of the public can rent it for holiday stays.

THE ROYAL
HOUSEHOLDS

OFFICES AND ROLES IN THE ROYAL HOUSEHOLD

The Queen's private secretary Edward Young (right), and her Equerry, Major Nana Kofi Twumasi-Ankrah, left, meet Boris Johnson (centre) at Buckingham Palace. December 2019. (PA Images)

Sir Michael Peat, the Keeper of the Privy Purse in 2001, in the boiler room of Buckingham Palace. (PA Images)

Members of the Royal Household who provide support to the Queen and members of the royal family are known as courtiers or 'royal aides'. They are based at Buckingham Palace, St James's Palace, Clarence House and Kensington Palace in London; Windsor Castle; and the Palace of Holyroodhouse in Edinburgh.

The Private Secretary's Office

This department supports the monarch in crucial constitutional, governmental and political duties as head of state.

- The monarch's private secretary is regarded as the sovereign's most senior adviser, someone who is privy to confidential information that is not even shared with a consort or spouse.
- The private secretary is supported by a deputy and at least one assistant private secretary. Every senior working member of the royal family is also served by a private secretary or a principal private secretary. They lead a department that organises domestic and overseas official programmes, as well as advising on constitutional matters and taking responsibility for everything from speeches and correspondence to official presents and congratulatory messages to members of the public.
- The communication secretary heads the Press Office and reports to the leading private secretary or, on occasion, to the monarch personally.
- Royal Communications (formerly Buckingham Palace Press Office) is responsible for making arrangements for members of the media, from newspapers to television news teams, to cover royal visits, royal engagements, major events such as births, deaths, marriages and jubilees, as well as ongoing news stories involving members of the royal family. They are tasked with providing accurate information

ELIZABETH'S PRIVATE SECRETARIES

The Queen has been served by nine private secretaries during her reign. They are:

ALAN LASCELLES *(1952–53; he also served George VI in the same role from 1943–52)*
MICHAEL ADEANE *(1952–72)*
MARTIN CHARTERIS *(1972–77)*
PHILIP MOORE *(1977–86)*
WILLIAM HESELTINE *(1986–90)*
ROBERT FELLOWES *(1990–99)*
ROBIN JANVRIN *(1999–2007)*
CHRISTOPHER GEIDT *(2007–17)*
EDWARD YOUNG *(2017–present)*

and responses to inquiries from across the world. They also distribute press releases, operational notes, speeches and annual financial reports.

ROYAL COMMUNICATIONS

In 2014, the palace press offices of members of the royal family were merged into one office based at Buckingham Palace under the supervision of the Director of Royal Communications, Ms Sally Osman. After Ms Osman left the role in 2018 the system was tweaked again and Donal McCabe, a senior corporate affairs professional, became communications secretary to the Queen. His team looks after media affairs for the Queen, the Duke of Edinburgh and all their children, with the exception of Prince Charles, and the Duke and Duchess of Cambridge, who have their own communications secretaries:

- Since 2016 Mr Julian Payne has led the Prince of Wales's public relations operation as communications secretary to the Prince of Wales and Duchess of Cornwall, and is based at Clarence House.
- Christian Jones, a former government speech writer, was appointed communications secretary to Prince William and the Duchess of Cambridge in March 2019.

The Privy Purse and Treasurer's Office

This department enables the Royal Household to operate as a business. It is worth noting that there really is a 'privy purse', which is made of tapestry. At the coronation, the department's head – known as the keeper of the privy purse – carries the purse in the ceremonial procession at Westminster Abbey; afterwards, it becomes his or her property. Traditionally, silver coins were kept in the purse for the keeper to

distribute to the poor en route to the coronation. In theory, these were handed out by the sovereign, but the keeper was expected to provide the coins from their own pocket. The custom has now lapsed.

The keeper is supported by a deputy and also a chief accountant and paymaster and is also responsible for the accounts of other households within the Royal Household, with the exception of that of Prince Charles. The keeper of the privy purse looks after the monarch's private financial affairs, too, and controls his or her bank account, which is held at Coutts (now part of the National Westminster Group) in The Strand.

The keeper of the purse is also responsible for the finances of royal estates, the royal stud and the monarch's racing expenses. The department

The Queen talks to Sir Simon Cooper (far right) Master of the Household from 1992 to 2000, at Buckingham Palace, at the Riding Masters, Quatermasters and Directors of Music Association reception at St James's Palace, June 2009. (PA Images)

supports functions such as finance, human resources, IT and telecoms, internal audit, and property services.

The Master of the Household's Department

The Household department deals with everything to do with the official and private entertaining in any of the royal residences, from housekeeping and catering to floristry and specialist craftspeople. The team is led by the Master of the Household, sometimes described as the country's most important housekeeper, and comprises more than 300 men and women staff with a diverse skillset.

The department came about thanks to the reforming zeal of Prince Albert, who wanted to break up the 'mini empires' he perceived were in place at the palace and instead put one person in charge of all domestic staff. Eventually, he persuaded Queen Victoria, who did not like change of any kind, to create the new position.

The Lord Chamberlain's Office

This department, led by the comptroller, is in charge of organising aspects of the Queen's programme that involve ceremonial activity or public-facing events, such as garden parties, state events, royal weddings or the State Opening of Parliament. They also manage the Royal Mews and arrangements for royal travel, as well as the awarding of honours.

The Lord Chamberlain himself is titular head of the Royal Household with overall responsibility of all of its departments; in theory at least, he is in charge of everything. The final decision for the appointment of the Lord Chamberlain rests with the Queen, after taking advice from a number of people, including senior politicians and senior members of her household. However, it was not until 1923, under the first Labour government led by Ramsay MacDonald, that the sovereign was given the right to make this choice; before then, the post was the choice of the government and a new Lord Chamberlain took office when each new government was formed.

Royal Collection Trust

This department is run by the director of the Royal Collection, who is responsible for the way it is presented to the public. The team is also responsible for the management of the public opening of the official residences of the Queen and Prince Charles. In recent years, the Trust's work has evolved to new areas such as conservation, scholarly publishing, digitisation, learning programmes and touring exhibitions. The current chairman of the management board is Tim Knox, director of The Royal Collection.

Camilla, Duchess of Cornwall, with Tony Johnstone-Burt (right, Master of the Household to the Queen), attending a reception for the London Taxi Drivers' Charity for Children at Buckingham Palace, February 2019. (PA Images)

PALACE JOBS AND STAFF SALARIES

Housekeeping assistant

The Royal Household recently advertised for housekeeping assistants, on a wage of just £8.17 an hour, £2.03 below the London Living Wage rate.

Butler

Back in 2011, Buckingham Palace advertised for a trainee butler with a starting salary of £15,000, with accommodation thrown in. Paul Burrell is perhaps the most famous royal butler, who was described by the late Princess Diana as her 'rock'.

Pot-washer

In 2016, Buckingham Palace advertised for somebody to do the dishes. The successful applicant receives an annual salary of £17,000 with a room on the grounds.

Assistant gardener

In 2018, Prince Edward and the Countess of Wessex needed somebody to work in the 21 hectare grounds of Bagshot Park, near Windsor. A salary of £18,000 for a 40-hour week was up for grabs, with lunch provided.

Groom

The royals have a long-standing love affair with all things equine, and in 2014 the Queen was looking for a groom to ride her beloved horses, train foals and muck out the stables, in return for a £20,000 salary.

Liveried helper

This position was based at the Royal Mews at Buckingham Palace. The successful applicant received £20,000 a year, plus 33 days' annual holiday and a 15 per cent employer's pension contribution. Applicants had to be 'highly capable' riders, willing to 'acquire knowledge of driving carriages and of state harnesses'.

Telephone operator

Given that Buckingham Palace has to field 7,000 calls a week, this would presumably be a fairly hectic job. A recent ad revealed it is one that would pay £23,000pa.

Business development and communications manager

When it was advertised the role was to provide maternity cover, but nevertheless came with a salary of £30–32,000 per annum, presumably depending on experience. The role involved persuading people to

visit 'one of the world's greatest and most diverse art collections' at Holyroodhouse Palace, where it is based.

Social media specialist

In this fast-changing world, the royal family has recognised the need to have a presence on Facebook, Twitter and Instagram. In 2016, a position to manage this aspect of the royals' lives came with a £50,000 salary. The job involved managing the royal pages and recruiting new followers, with the advertisement adding: 'It's about never standing still and finding new ways to maintain the Queen's presence in the public eye and on the world stage.'

Master of the Household

Moving up the scale, the previous incumbent of the role, Air Marshal Sir David Walker, was reported to earn £122,000 per year. Responsibilities included managing the domestic staff in the kitchens, pages, footmen, and the housekeeper and her staff.

Private secretary to the Queen

The last private secretary, Sir Christopher Geidt, was reported to have had his annual salary frozen at £146,000 per year, plus perks.

Royal Collection Trust members of staff put the finishing touches to a 5m (15 ft) Christmas tree in the Crimson Drawing Room at Windsor Castle, Berkshire. (PA Images)

ODD JOBS

There are some interesting and unique roles in the Royal Household that date back as far as medieval times. Here are just a few.

The lord high almoner

He or she heads up the Royal Almonry, a small office dating from 1103 that is responsible for distributing alms to the poor. The post is usually a diocesan bishop or high cleric of the Church of England.

Warden of the swans

The role of swan warden was created in 1993 when the ancient post of keeper of the king's swans (which dated from the 13th century) was divided into two new posts. The first and so far only person to have this job is Professor Christopher Perrins LVO.

Marker of the swans

This is the other new role that was created when the keeper of the king's swans was divided into two posts. Under the new title, the swan marker arranges the annual event of Swan Upping on the River Thames and advises organisations throughout the country about swan welfare and incidents involving swans. In essence, he or she monitors the health of the local swan population and advises fishing and boating bodies on how to work with wildlife. The current office-holder is David Barber MVO, a boat engine merchant by occupation who was appointed in 1993. In accordance with tradition, he wears a scarlet rowing shirt and a special hat adorned with a white swan's feather to distinguish him from the other swan uppers.

The King's/Queen's bargemaster

Until the mid-19th century, the royal family commonly used the River Thames for transport, so a bargemaster – a post created in 1215 – would have been an essential member of staff. The holder of the post, which is now largely ceremonial, has since 2018 been Chris Livett. He is responsible for the 24 Royal Watermen who are paid the princely annual sum of £3.50. These are chosen from the ranks of the Thames Watermen – people who are licensed to operate tugs and launches on the river.

Duties include taking part in ceremonial events, both on the water and on land. For example, at the coronation, the Royal Watermen walk in the procession behind the Queen's bargemaster. At the State Opening of Parliament, the Queen's bargemaster and four Royal Watermen travel as boxmen on coaches. They also serve as footmen on royal carriages at other events, such as jubilees, weddings and funerals, and during state visits.

Piper to the Queen

The Queen has her own bagpiper. His official title is the Piper to the Sovereign, a position that has been filled in the Royal Household since 1843, apart from during a four-year gap during World War II. Only 15 people have held the title since its creation. The title-holder is responsible for playing the bagpipes whenever the Queen requests it.

Below: Swan uppers tag and record swans along the River Thames, between Marlow and Henley in Buckinghamshire, July 2017. (PA Images)

Below right: Jim Motherwell, the Queen's piper in 2002, plays ahead of the Queen Mother's coffin as it is carried out of the Royal Chapel of All Saints in Windsor Great Park before its journey to the Queen's Chapel at St James's Palace in London. (PA Images)

LADIES- AND LORDS-IN-WAITING

Did you know?

The highest ranking lady-in-waiting is Mistress of the Robes, second is Lady of the Bedchamber, last in the pecking order is Maid of Honour.

have a wretched woman talking away, so I would keep my mouth shut.' In 2017, the Queen appointed Lady Elizabeth Leeming and Mrs Simon Rhodes to be extra ladies-in-waiting.

Lords-in-waiting

These are personal appointments of the Queen from the most senior retired members of the Royal Household. They are always peers, and do not speak or vote against the government. In March 2019 the Queen's long-serving former private secretary, Lord Geidt, was appointed permanent lord-in-waiting. A permanent lord-in-waiting may also represent the sovereign, as often happens at funerals or memorial services for former courtiers. There is a separate political category of lord-in-waiting, who is appointed by the government of the day and serves as a junior government whip in the House of Lords.

Ladies-in-waiting

The role of lady-in-waiting is an ancient one that dates back to medieval times. Essentially, the role involves high-ranking noblewomen serving the Queen at court.

The current ladies-in-waiting are six aristocratic ladies who are a cross between friends and assistants to the Queen. Among the ladies to serve are three who have been ladies-in-waiting for more than 50 years: Lady Susan Hussey; Dame Mary Morrison, who has also been lady of the bedchamber since 1960; and Fortune FitzRoy, the Duchess of Grafton, who has been mistress of the robes since 1967. Another, the Countess of Airlie, is an American, who is also a lady of the bedchamber.

These women are in tune with the Queen and know when she is ready to move along. The cues are subtle, the result of learning to read her over many years. Riding in the car with the Queen, they let her take the conversational lead. 'She would have to be thinking about what to do, whom to meet, giving speeches,' recalled Esme, the Dowager Countess of Cromer, who was appointed in 1967. 'It would drive her mad to

Meghan, the Duchess of Sussex accompanied by Lord Christopher Geidt, the Queen's permanent lord-in-waiting, arrives to attend a panel discussion, convened by The Queen's Commonwealth Trust, to mark International Women's Day at King's College London, 8 March 2019. (Getty)

ROYAL
TRANSPORT

GLOBAL TRAVELLERS

The Queen has visited 120 out of the world's 196 countries, sailed more than 1.6 million km (1 million miles) on the Royal Yacht *Britannia* and travelled the equivalent of 42 times around the globe.

Financing royal travel

Royal travel is an extremely expensive business. For the year up to 31 March 2019, for example, the total cost of the royal family's travel came to £2.7 million, as revealed in the Sovereign Grant Report. Of that, nearly half had been spent on Prince Charles's visits abroad with the Duchess of Cornwall on behalf of the government, an increase of about one-third on the previous year. The majority of these saw the Prince of Wales visits travelling by chartered flight while his staff flew on scheduled flights. According to the report, all overseas visits funded by the Sovereign Grant are determined by the Foreign and Commonwealth Office and approved by the Royal Visits Committee.

Charles and Camilla are not alone in spending vast sums on official overseas visits, though: Prince Harry and Duchess of Sussex's visit to Australia, New Zealand, Tonga and Fiji in 2018 cost £81,000, and Prince William's visit to Jordan, Israel and the Palestinian occupied territories came in at £74,000.

The Queen waves as she boards her plane to leave Australia, March 2006 in Melbourne. (Getty)

The Queen II walks down the platform of Liverpool Lime railway station after disembarking the Royal Train on 22 June 2016. (Getty)

By land, sea and air

The Queen and the royal family complete more than 3,000 official engagements in the UK and abroad on behalf of the charitable organisations of which they are patrons, and as super ambassadors for Her Majesty's government. These visits require detailed planning – including reconnaissance visits by palace staff and security from Scotland Yard to ensure that nothing goes wrong. They prepare detailed notes for the member of the royal family carrying out the specific duty.

During her 63 years as monarch, the Queen has reached her destinations by land, sea and air – but in the past it would have been unthinkable for a monarch or senior royals to use public transport. As time has passed, though, royalty has been expected to conform and accept that if there is a cheaper option that is still safe, they may have to use it.

Wherever possible, therefore, the Queen has shown that she is happy to embrace change as long as it does not reduce the standing of the monarchy of which she is custodian. Royal travel is, after all, linked to the pomp and pageantry so closely associated with royal traditions. Priceless, gilded horse-drawn carriages used for ceremonial occasions and impressive state cars all add to the splendour and spectacle of monarchy.

Travelling by rail

It seems extraordinary to some that the Queen takes a public train, albeit in First Class. It's hard to imagine any sitting US president following Her Majesty's example. In recent years, her journey from London to Sandringham has become an annual event, travelling from London's Kings Cross station to King's Lynn in Norfolk en route to her Norfolk country estate.

Using scheduled train services has been introduced by the keeper of the privy purse in a bid to drive costs down. He has the task of getting the balance right so that the sovereign and her family travel in a cost-effective manner, but also in a style befitting their status. It is a tricky job, as royal accounts are scrutinised annually by the media and transport is always an area that comes in for particular criticism.

THE ROYAL CARS

In 1896, Edward VII, when he was still Prince of Wales, became the first royal to drive a car, during a demonstration of one of the first Daimlers in the Science Museum in London. Cars soon became his passion and he immediately ordered a Daimler for himself, although he never learned to drive properly, preferring to leave it to his personal chauffeur and mechanic, C.W. Stamper.

There is no record of whether George V could drive, but later monarchs Edward VIII and George VI certainly did. The Queen also enjoys driving, thanks in part to experiences doing so during her time in the Auxiliary Territorial Service during World War II. She is the only person in the UK who is permitted to drive without a driving licence. Since the 1950s, she has regularly been spotted as either the passenger or driver of a Land Rover, although these days she tends to restrict her time behind the wheel to when she is driving around her private estates.

For official duties – providing transport for state and other visitors as well as the Queen herself – there are eight state limousines, consisting of two Bentleys, three Rolls-Royces and three Daimlers. Other vehicles in the royal fleet include a number of Volkswagen people carriers. They are painted in a special royal claret-and-black livery and the state vehicles do not have registration number plates.

THE PHANTOMS

The oldest car in the fleet is the Phantom IV. Built in 1950, this has a 5.76 litre straight-eight engine and a Mulliner body. Princess Elizabeth and the Duke of Edinburgh used it before Elizabeth became queen. Despite its age, the car is in fine condition and is still used for occasions such as Ascot.

THE ROYAL MEWS

The Royal Mews is the place where the state cars are kept at Buckingham Palace. It is open to the public throughout the year and receives thousands of visitors.

The Queen inspects the new Bentley State Limousine car presented to her as a golden jubilee gift on behalf of a consortium of British-based automotive manufacturing and service companies. The car has been fully fitted to withstand terrorist attacks. (PA Images)

What's more, the Society of Motor Manufacturers and Traders presented a Rolls-Royce Phantom VI to the Queen for her Silver Jubilee in 1977, and there is also a 1986 Phantom VI.

Bentley State Limousine

VITAL STATISTICS

YEAR MADE: *2002*
SIZE: *6.22m (20.4ft) long with a wheelbase of 3.84m (12.6ft), 2m (6.6ft) wide, 1.77m (5.8ft) high*
COLOUR: *Royal claret and black*
ENGINE: *400bhp Bentley L series 6.75 litre V8 with twin turbochargers*
MAXIMUM SPEED: *209km/h (130mph)*
ESTIMATED WORTH: *£10 million*

The most frequently used form of transport for the monarch is a chauffeur-driven State Limousine, which is used for public engagements and some ceremonial occasions. These magnificent vehicles are designed so that the public can get the best view possible of the Queen. She has two Bentleys, the first presented to her for her Golden Jubilee in 2002. The one-off design, conceived by a Bentley-led consortium of British motor industry manufacturers and suppliers, was created with specific input from the Queen and Prince Philip, as well as her head chauffeur.

The plush interior of the Queen's Bentley State Limousine, May 2002. (PA Images)

CONSTRUCTION
The special Bentley cars have a modern monocoque construction – created as a single shell, rather than built up on a chassis – that maximises the car's interior space. Both Bentleys are 6.22m (20.4ft) long, nearly 1m (3.3ft) longer than a standard Bentley Arnage. At 3.84m (12.6ft), the wheelbase is 1.3m (4.3ft) longer than that of an average family-sized saloon. The rear doors are hinged at the back and are designed to allow the Queen to stand up straight before stepping down to the ground.

The Bentleys are fitted with a removable exterior roof covering that exposes a clear inner lining, giving an all-round view of their royal passengers. There are also extra security features, such as armoured bodywork and glass, a cabin that can be sealed in case of gas attack, and Kevlar-reinforced tyres.

SPEED
The Bentleys, like any other cars, are subject to normal speed restrictions despite having extremely powerful engines – Bentley L series 6.75 litre V8 with twin turbochargers. During royal processional occasions, they travel at around 14.5kph (9mph), and sometimes as slow as 4.8km (3mph).

UPHOLSTERY
The rear seats are upholstered in Hield Lambswool Sateen cloth, while all remaining upholstery is in light grey Connolly hide. Carpets are pale blue in the rear and dark blue in the front.

Bentley Bentayga

VITAL STATISTICS

YEAR MADE: *2016*
SIZE: *5.14m (16.86ft) long, 1.99m (6.53ft) wide, 1.74m (5.71ft) high*
COLOUR: *Not known*
ENGINE: *600bhp W12-power*
SPEED: *301km/h (187mph)*
ESTIMATED VALUE: *£229,000 (£500,000 including the Breitling Tourbillon clock on the dashboard)*

The Queen became the first to own the new Bentley Bentayga in 2015, the fastest and most powerful SUV in the world. 'We have reserved the number one car for her', Bentley CEO Wolfgang Duerheime said at the 2015 Frankfurt Motor Show. He said the Queen would be able to spec her own car.

Range Rover LWB Landaulet

VITAL STATISTICS

YEAR MADE: *2015*

SIZE: *5.2m (17ft) long, 1.99m (6.53ft) wide, 1.84m (6.04ft) high*

COLOUR: *Royal claret*

Engine: 565bhp 5.0L V8 Supercharged SVAutobiography Dynamic

SPEED: *250km/h (155mph)*

ESTIMATED VALUE: *The entry-level model costs £160,200, but the Queen's is worth rather more*

The Queen's version of this hybrid Range Rover SUV is based on a long wheelbase Range Rover, and has been modified to include backward-opening doors and an open-air top so that she can stand up in the vehicle and wave to the crowds. Another evident modification made specially for the Queen is the royal flag mounted on the car's bonnet. As for all the cars in the fleet, it is likely that there are other secret safety features, such a bullet-proof glass, but details of these are not publicised.

Land Rover Defender

VITAL STATISTICS

YEAR MADE: *2002*

SIZE: *3.88m (12.73ft) long, 1.79m (5.87ft) wide, 2.06m (6.76ft) high*

ENGINE SIZE: *4.2 V8 engine*

COLOUR: *Green*

SPEED: *130km/h (81mph)*

ESTIMATED WORTH: *Sold at auction for £30,240*

Production of the Defender came to halt in 2016, but the series remain among the Queen's favourites in the fleet. She now leases the vehicles and hands them back after a few years. Like all her cars, the Defender had special royal specification and extras such as heated seats, electric windows and slightly raised suspension to make it easier for her to drive it across her estates, such as at Sandringham. The 2002 Defender that the Queen sold at auction had custom green leather.

Rolls-Royce Silver Jubilee Phantom VI

VITAL STATISTICS

YEAR MADE: *1977*

SIZE: *6m (19.7ft) long, 2m (6.56ft) wide,*

1.8m (5.9ft) high

COLOUR: *Royal claret and black*

ENGINE: *6,230cc V8*

ESTIMATED VALUE: *A similar one had a guide price of £400,000–600,000*

The Queen, in a Land Rover Defender 110, drives to the stables on the Sandringham Estate, Norfolk. January 2000. (PA Images)

The two Rolls-Royce Phantom VIs were the official state cars until they were replaced in the order of precedence in 2002 by the two Bentleys. Both are nearly identical from the outside apart from the fact that the 1977 version has a slightly higher roof. This vehicle was presented to the Queen by the British motor industry to celebrate her 25th jubilee in 1977, and it was the car that carried Kate Middleton to her wedding in 2011.

Rolls-Royce Phantom VI

VITAL STATISTICS

YEAR MADE: *1950*

SIZE: *5.77m (18.9ft) long, 1.95m (6.4ft) wide, 1.88m (6.2ft) high*

COLOUR: *Originally Valentine green (deep green with a slight blue secondary hue) with red belt-line striping. When it became a state car in 1952, it was repainted royal claret and black*

ENGINE: *6.5L*

ESTIMATED VALUE: *A similar one had a guide price of about £2 million*

This is a more conventional model of the 1977 version. Like all British state cars, the Phantom VIs have a special mount for a Royal Standard and coat of arms. When

The Queen and Prince Philip make their way down the Mall in an open-topped Range Rover, during the Patron's Lunch in central London in honour of the Queen's 90th birthday. (PA Images)

the Queen is a passenger, the Spirit of Ecstasy bonnet sculpture is replaced by a unique silver model of St George slaying the dragon, and the registration number plates are removed.

Rolls-Royce Phantom IV

VITAL STATISTICS

YEAR MADE: *1986*
SIZE: *6m long (19.7ft), 2m (6.56ft) wide, 1.8m (5.9ft) high*
COLOUR: *Royal claret and black*
ENGINE: *6,750 cc, V8*
ESTIMATED VALUE: *A similar one had a guide price of £400,000–600,000*

Rolls-Royce only made 18 of these vehicles between 1950 and 1956. They were intended for buyers whom Rolls-Royce considered worthy, including the British royal family and heads of state. Sixteen are currently known to still exist in museums as well as in public and private collections. The special body for the car was made by H.J. Mulliner & Co – the first example of this model that was built. When the car was completed in July 1950 its delivery was accompanied by a public announcement stating the Phantom IV had been 'designed to the special order of Their Royal Highnesses, the Princess Elizabeth and the Duke of Edinburgh'. It had an automatic gearbox fitted in 1955.

It is still occasionally used for royal and state occasions. For example, it was used at William and Kate's wedding to carry the Prince of Wales and the Duchess of Cornwall from Clarence House to Westminster Abbey. In 2018 it brought Meghan to St George's Chapel, Windsor, for her marriage to Harry.

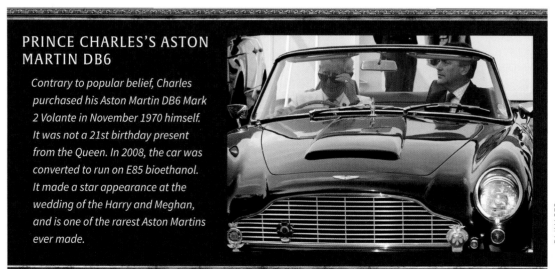

PRINCE CHARLES'S ASTON MARTIN DB6

Contrary to popular belief, Charles purchased his Aston Martin DB6 Mark 2 Volante in November 1970 himself. It was not a 21st birthday present from the Queen. In 2008, the car was converted to run on E85 bioethanol. It made a star appearance at the wedding of the Harry and Meghan, and is one of the rarest Aston Martins ever made.

PA IMAGES

COACHES

THE GOLD STATE COACH
VITAL STATISTICS

YEAR: *1762*
SIZE: *3.6m (11.8ft) high and over 7m (23ft) long*
WEIGHT: *4 tonnes*
ESTIMATED WORTH: *Commissioned for £7,562 (around £1.5 million today), but it is impossible to guess what it is worth today.*

A collection of historic carriages and coaches is housed in the Royal Mews at Buckingham Palace, most of which are still in use.

The centrepiece of the Royal Mews exhibition is the stunning Gold State Coach, which has featured in every coronation since George IV's in 1821. The coach was originally built for George III for his coronation in 1760, and for his wedding to Princess Charlotte of Mecklenburg-Strelitz, but it was not ready in time; the first occasion he used it was when he travelled to Westminster to open Parliament on 25 November 1762.

The exterior of the coach is covered with gold leaf and lavishly decorated. In addition to panels painted by Battista Cipriani, there are symbolic motifs in the form of gilded sculptures – three cherubs on the roof of the carriage and four tritons, one on each corner – and elaborate carvings of crowns, palm trees, lions' heads, faces and dolphins. The interior is richly upholstered with velvet and satin. The coach is drawn by eight horses (always Windsor greys), which are postilion ridden in four pairs. Accompanying them on foot are nine grooms, six footmen and four Yeomen of the Guard, as well as the royal coachman, who rides at the front of the carriage.

Irish State Coach

This coach is the one most often seen in public, as it is used for the State Opening of Parliament. It was originally built in 1851 and given as a gift by the Lord Mayor of Dublin, who was also a coachbuilder. The exterior is blue and black with gilt decoration, and the interior is blue damask. It is driven from the box seat with four horses.

Other coaches include:
- Scottish State Coach (built in 1830 and used for Scottish and English processions)
- Queen Alexandra's State Coach (used to take the Imperial State crown to Parliament for state openings)
- 1902 State Landau, used for WIlliam's wedding.
- Australian State Coach (presented to the Queen in 1988 by Australia to mark its bicentenary)
- Glass Coach (built in 1881 and traditionally used for royal weddings)
- State and semi-state landaus used in state processions

In addition, there are two barouches, broughams (which still carry messengers on their official rounds in London), and Queen Victoria's ivory-mounted phaeton (used by the Queen since 1987 for her birthday parade).

The Queen and Prince Philip leaving Buckingham Palace in the Gold State Coach with a yeomen escort on their way to St Paul's Cathedral for a service to mark the Golden Jubilee. (Getty)

Left: Carriage cleaners Richard Borer (left) and Christopher Drewitt, buff up the State Landaus at the Royal Mews in central London, in preparation for the Golden Jubilee celebrations, May 2002.

THE BRITISH ROYAL TRAIN

The sitting room of Queen's saloon on board the royal train as they looked when first fitted out in the 1970s. (PA Images)

The British royal train comes with chefs, lace-trimmed pillows, and an unbreakable rule that no bumpy track should be encountered during the Queen's 7.30am bath. It is fitted with modern communications facilities as well, and acts as an essential mobile office when the Queen is on her 'away days' in specific regions across the country.

Only the Queen, Prince Philip and Prince Charles use the royal train. It enables them to travel overnight and at times when the weather is too bad to fly, and to work and hold meetings during lengthy journeys. Royal train journeys are always arranged so as not to interfere with scheduled train services.

History

On 13 June 1842, Queen Victoria took the very first royal train journey, from Slough to Paddington, London. It lasted a mere 25 minutes and was made in a train that comprised the engine *Phlegethon*, pulling the royal saloon and six other carriages.

The earliest carriages date back to the same period, and multiple sets of these were kept in different regions for local use up until 1977. The current rolling stock dates from the late 1970s and early 1980s, and it wasn't until the 1990s that dedicated locomotives in special livery appeared, although the carriages are also sometimes pulled by steam on special occasions.

The carriages

Carriages are maroon in colour and have red-and-black coach lining and a grey roof. They consist of the royal compartments, sleeping, dining and support cars.

The Queen's saloon contains a bedroom, bathroom and sitting room and has an entrance that opens directly on to the platform. The Duke of Edinburgh's saloon has a similar layout, with the addition of a kitchen. Hanging in both saloons are Scottish landscapes by Roy Penny and Victorian prints of earlier rail journeys. In the Duke of Edinburgh's saloon there is also a piece of Brunel's original broad-gauge rail, which was presented on the 150th anniversary of the Great Western Railway; Brunel had accompanied Queen Victoria on her inaugural train journey in 1842.

The two saloons came into service in 1977, when they were extensively used during the Silver Jubilee royal tours. The saloons had started out in 1972 as prototypes for the standard InterCity Mark III passenger carriage and were later fitted out for their royal role at the Wolverton depot, where work on the royal train is normally done.

THE COST OF COMFORT

Prince Charles travels more than other members of the royal family as he undertakes visits on behalf of the Queen now that she is advancing in years. This brings the total cost of Charles' rail trips to a huge sum. For example, Charles took an individual trip to Wales in December 2018 by Royal Train that cost £17,000, while an individual visit to Scotland in January 2019 came to the same sum. Another lone visit to Wales in February 2019 by Prince Charles cost £20,000.

FLYING HIGH

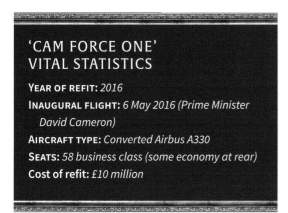

'CAM FORCE ONE'
VITAL STATISTICS

YEAR OF REFIT: *2016*

INAUGURAL FLIGHT: *6 May 2016 (Prime Minister David Cameron)*

AIRCRAFT TYPE: *Converted Airbus A330*

SEATS: *58 business class (some economy at rear)*

Cost of refit: *£10 million*

The royal family have used planes to get them to destinations for royal visits since Edward VIII became the first British monarch to fly in 1936. Since then, flying has become the primary means of long-distance transport, and has allowed the Queen to visit many more places than any of her predecessors.

The Royal Travel Office, which is based at Buckingham Palace, is in charge of coordinating the use of the different types of aircraft by members of the royal family. The cost is met by the annual Royal Travel Grant-in-aid provided by the Department for Transport.

The King's Flight

The formalisation of royal flying occurred on 21 July 1936 when the King's Flight, based at Hendon in North London, was formed. The first aircraft was the king's own private plane, the twin-engine Dragon Rapide, G-ADDD. However, the following year an Airspeed Envoy III G-AEXX was purchased – the first aircraft bought for the King's Flight.

The King's Flight was disbanded during World War II, with royals instead using military aircraft as a mode of transport. Then, in 1946, it was reformed in greater strength at RAF Benson and consisted of four Vickers Vikings. These were subsequently used for the royal tour of South Africa the following year.

The Queen's Flight

After the Queen came to the throne, the group became known as the Queen's Flight and acquired many different types of aircraft, both for transporting royals and

teaching them to fly. This continued a precedent that had been set by King Edward VIII when he was the Prince of Wales: he had learned to fly in France during World War I, and continued to fly after the war.

Many other members of the royal family since then have learned to fly, including Prince Philip and Prince Charles. Both Prince William and Prince Harry are also qualified plane and helicopter pilots.

Aircraft used for the official flying of members of the royal family have included BAe 146 and HS 125 jet aircraft of 32 (The Royal) Squadron. This is based at RAF Northolt, north-west of London, and was formed from the former 32 Squadron after a merger with the Queen's Flight in 1995. Squadron aircraft have a white livery with a red, white and red stripe.

Royals have also used a Sikorsky S-76 C+ helicopter that is operated by the Royal Household from Blackbushe Aerodrome in Hampshire. This is finished in the red and blue colours of the Brigade of Guards.

In 2014, the Queen leased an £8 million helicopter for members of the royal family to use on official engagements. The luxury AgustaWestland AW109S Grand comes complete with leather seat covering and customised interior, and is used by royals on official visits. The switch to the helicopter was the result of a safety scare in 2013 when Charles and Camilla were forced to make an emergency landing in the old

The interior of the BOAC DC-7C in which the Queen and Prince Philip flew from London to Ottawa at the beginning of their Canadian tour in October 1957. (Getty)

The Prince of Wales and Duchess of Cornwall made history on 25 March 2019, when they arrived in Havana, Cuba for the first-ever official visit to the country by members of the British royal family. Their two-day stopover was part of a nearly two-week tour of the Caribbean. (Jobson Media)

Prince William and the Duchess of Cambridge walk down the steps of RAF Voyager as they arrive in Lahore, at the start of their royal visit to Pakistan, October 2019. Later, the plane carrying them back from Lahore to Islamabad had to turn back after two aborted landings due to a thunderstorm. (PA Images)

helicopter when it was on its way to the Hay-on-Wye festival in Wales. The new helicopter, made by Anglo-Italian company AgustaWestland – a first for the Queen, whose earlier helicopters have all been American Sikorskys – is based alongside the Queen's other private helicopter at RAF Odiham in Hampshire.

Cam Force One

The primary role of 32 (The Royal) Squadron is to provide support in operational theatres for the Ministry of Defence. Spare capacity on the aircraft is offered to the royal family, the prime minister and senior ministers.

In 2016, the RAF unveiled a refitted jet that provides VIP transport for government ministers and the royal family – and that came with a price tag of £10 million. Ministers justified the cost by saying that the conversion would save the taxpayer £775,000 a year in private charters, and that the aircraft would still be available for its primary air-to-air refuelling role when it is not being used for transporting royals and ministers.

The converted RAF Voyager is nicknamed 'Cam Force One' as it was UK PM David Cameron who sanctioned it – a play on the name of America's presidential jet, Air Force One. It flies incumbent prime ministers to important summits as well as the most senior royals, such as Charles (and sometimes Prince William), on official business abroad on behalf of the Queen. Priority is given to the head of state but as she no longer undertakes long-distance travel, she has not used it.

The aircraft, based on the Airbus A330, has been fitted with 58 business seats. The Ministry of Defence said the new seating would allow the aircraft, based at RAF Brize Norton in Oxfordshire, to transport large business delegations when travelling on important prime ministerial visits, such as to India and China.

Did you know?

Prince William was just nine months old when he was taken on his first overseas trip, an official trip to Australia and New Zealand in 1983. At the time, it was not usual for royal children to accompany their parents on tour, but Diana, Princess of Wales decided that he should come too.

THE ROYAL YACHT *BRITANNIA*

The Royal Yacht Britannia's dining room, set for guests, after the vessel's major refit in August 1973. (PA Images)

H er Majesty's Yacht (HMY) *Britannia* was the monarch's floating home during many UK and overseas tours for 44 years, and the internationally recognised flagship of Great Britain.

History

Built by the Scotland's shipbuilders John Brown & Co at a cost of £2,098,000 to replace her 50-year-old predecessor, HMY *Victoria and Albert*, HMY *Britannia* was named and launched by the Queen on 16 April 1953 and was commissioned on 11 January 1954.

The royal yacht was subsequently a highly successful venue for official entertaining and receptions, as well as a residence for royal tours. It provided state apartments catering for up to 250 guests, and included office space and accommodation for the royal family and staff.

The royal yacht *Britannia* was decommissioned in 1997 and is now a floating museum in Leith, Scotland owned and cared for by The Royal Yacht *Britannia* Trust.

Fixtures and fittings

the yacht was a treasure trove of royal objects. *Britannia's* state apartments contained furniture and recycled fittings from HMY *Victoria and Albert*, including a table designed by Prince Albert. The wheel in the wheelhouse was from George V's racing yacht *Britannia*, while the binnacle on the veranda deck was first used on the *Royal George* (built in 1817) and fitted in each successive royal yacht. Other family memorabilia included Prince Philip's collection of driftwood.

The yacht had three masts: a 41m (133ft) foremast, a 42m (139ft) mainmast and a 36m (118ft) mizzenmast. The top aerial on the foremast and the top 6.1m (20ft) of the mainmast were hinged so that the ship could pass under bridges. Royal yachtsmen, who were all volunteers from the General Service of the Royal Navy, were distinguished by their uniform. Hand signals were used in place of shouted orders, with written daily orders instead of a broadcast system.

VITAL STATISTICS

SHIPBUILDER: *John Brown & Co*
LAUNCH DATE: *16 April 1953*
COMMISSION DATE: *11 January 1954*
MEASUREMENTS: *126m (412ft)*
TONNAGE: *5,769 GT*
CREW: *21 officers, 250 Royal Yachtsmen*
TROOPS: *1 platoon of Royal Marines*
COST: *£2,098,000*

A MUCH-LOVED FLOATING HOME

To the royal family, HMY Britannia was much more than a ship or a means of transport; she was their floating home, a vessel full of private memories where they could be themselves. During the decommissioning ceremony the Queen wept openly – a highly unusual show of emotion.

Sir Donald Gosling, founder of National Car Parks, left the royal family £50 million in his will when he died in September 2019 in order to replace the Royal Yacht Britannia. He had previously attempted to raise £60 million for a new yacht to replace the Britannia in 1994.

LEISURE,
PASTIMES
AND PETS

THE QUEEN'S YEAR

For all the adaptations that the Palace has had to make as it responds to modern life, the Queen's diary is still worked out according to a set pattern that has remained largely unchanged for years.

December–February

The Queen's year begins at Sandringham, in Norfolk, where the royal family gathers for the Christmas and New Year break. Life here is a little less formal, and there are numerous shooting parties. The Queen first visited Sandringham as a baby, and is deeply attached to it. One aspect in which she takes a particular interest is the Sandringham kennels; all of the puppies born there are named by the Queen personally. When she's not there or at the stud, she loves to pop into the royal pigeon lofts, which house about 240 birds, many of which regularly win national and international races. While younger members come and go, the Queen and the Duke of Edinburgh remain at Sandringham until early February.

February–Easter

Since his retirement at the age of 96, Prince Philip has spent most of his time at Wood Farm on the Sandringham Estate. The Queen, meanwhile, returns to Buckingham Palace until Easter,

Easter–June

Windsor Castle is the focal point for several highlights of the Queen's calendar. These include family Easter celebrations, the Garter Ceremony – when members of the Order of the Garter gather – and Royal Ascot.

June–July

The Queen takes up residence at the Palace of Holyroodhouse in Edinburgh in June for a week of engagements, called 'Holyrood Week' or 'Royal Week', depending on which side of the border you're from. After that, she returns to London until early August.

August

The Queen and Prince Philip go to Scotland at the beginning of August to spend the rest of the summer at Balmoral. The deer, grouse and salmon provide fine game and the setting, among the pine forests of Deeside, is spectacular. Once a year the Queen invites the British prime minister and his or her spouse for a late-summer's weekend at Balmoral. There are picnics and barbecues – with Prince Philip sometimes acting as chef – after which the Queen has been known to do the washing up by hand.

September–December

The Queen does not return from Balmoral until September, when she resumes formal royal duties, visiting individual organisations for a particular event or on one of her so-called 'away days' to a particular city or county. Every couple of years the Queen hosts visiting dignitaries on incoming state visits. The State Opening of Parliament ceremony in front of both Houses usually takes place in November.

State events

As head of state, the Queen must frequently leave her country pursuits behind and don her grand apparel for a number of set-piece events, such as the two incoming state visits that she hosts each year. The pomp and circumstance accorded to the arrival of presidents or

> **Did you know?**
> Every summer while on holiday at Balmoral the Queen holds two Ghillies' Balls – to which she invites estate workers, castle staff, neighbours and members of the local community.

Charles and Anne watch with their mother, the Queen, unpack a basket of goods onto the stall at which she was serving in a sale of work at Abergeldie Castle, near Balmoral. The sale was organised to help raise funds for building a vestry at Crathie Church, where the Royal family attend when at Balmoral. August 1955. (PA Images)

The Queen and Prince Philip lead out other members of the family with Reverend Canon Jonathan Riviere as they leave the traditional Christmas Day church service at St Mary Magdalene Church in Sandringham, 2017. (Getty)

visiting royalty is always impressive and few could fail to be uplifted by a journey in one of the famous state coaches, or by the sheer scale of the banquet that is held in their honour.

Faith and charity

Throughout her long reign, the Queen has been guided by her deep religious faith. As monarch, she is also supreme governor of the Church of England – and it is a role she takes seriously. Wherever she is, she likes to attend church on Sundays and those who know her say her faith gives her an inner calm. Every Christmas, her broadcasts both at home and abroad contain overtly Christian messages. It may be unfashionable, but it is heartfelt and fiercely traditional, in keeping with the Queen's profound beliefs.

Another important aspect of her life is the support she can give to charities and other organisations by accepting a role as patron. Currently, she is linked to more than 600 – including many military associations, the children's charity NSPCC, the Kennel Club and the Campaign to Protect Rural England. Clearly, she cannot

be directly involved in all of them, but merely having the Queen as patron provides vital publicity for the work of these organisations, and allows their achievements and contributions to society to be recognised.

RED BOXES

Wherever she goes, the Queen's work goes with her. Each evening, the famous hand-crafted leather 'Red Box' or despatch box (made by Barrow Hepburn & Gale) arrives for her perusal. A symbol of the democratic system of government, the despatch boxes ensure the secure transportation of sensitive documents that impact the UK and its relations with other countries. Much of the correspondence inside the box is dense parliamentary business, but the Queen is assiduous about reading and returning it by the following morning. At weekends, she is sent a larger selection, including a summary of events around the Commonwealth. The Queen also presides over regular meetings of the Privy Council at which routine government business is quickly dealt with, freeing up Parliament to concentrate on more complex matters.

FAMILY LIFE

The Queen and Prince Philip are joined by their family at Clarence House for a dinner to mark their diamond wedding anniversary in November 2007. (PA Images)

In addition to being the reigning monarch, the Queen is of course also head of a very large family, and a wife, mother, grandmother, great-grandmother, and friend to a very select group.

Prince Philip, Duke of Edinburgh

Elizabeth's marriage to Prince Philip has been the bedrock of every aspect of her life. She fell for the handsome sailor when she was just 13 and married him when she was 21. She has always used her feminine wiles to placate the occasionally temperamental Philip. At home, she lets him wear the trousers: running the estates, making the big decisions and sometimes bossing her about. He is, after all, the only one who would dare. Since his retirement, though, Philip sees less of the Queen now he is based at Wood Farm on the Sandringham estate most of the time.

The Queen and Prince Philip are not the sort of couple to show their emotions in public but, in a speech on their golden wedding anniversary, the Queen put her feelings on record: 'Prince Philip,' she said, 'is someone who doesn't take easily to compliments but he has, quite simply, been my strength and stay all these years. And I owe him a debt greater than he would ever claim, or we shall ever know.'

Mother

As a mother, the Queen's life has been more troubled. With three divorces and two remarriages between her four children, the Queen has had to steer a careful path through the minefield of extended family relations. She is an intensely private person and to see her children's marital squabbles making newspaper headlines has been traumatic, yet she rarely intervenes.

The scars, perhaps, run deepest in her relationship with Prince Charles and there's often an awkwardness when they are together. However, at one of Charles's birthday parties, he made it clear that he admires her as a mother and as sovereign. 'Mummy', he said to peals of laughter – 'coupled, of course, with Your Majesty. I don't quite know how you've put up with me for all these years!'

Grandmother

It must be strange to have to bow or curtsey to your grandmother, but all of the Queen's grandchildren have been brought up to respect the institution she embodies, as well as to love their granny. However, unlike everyone else, they all bow or curtsey only once a day, on their first meeting.

The Queen is an important figure in all their lives, from the eldest Peter Phillips to the youngest James, Viscount Severn. But none depends on her wisdom and experience as much as Prince William, who will one day take on the same weighty role as monarch. William says his relationship with his grandmother is going from

GOING INCOGNITO

Even the monarch can go undercover sometimes. On a trip to Scotland, she got into conversation with some American tourists while walking. Asked if she lived in the area, Elizabeth mentioned that she had a house nearby, and when asked if she'd ever met the Queen she simply pointed at her policeman and said, 'No, but he has!'

strength to strength as he gets older. She's always keen for him to ask questions and he says there's nothing she won't already know, or have a better opinion about.

A SPECIAL RELATIONSHIP

William towers over his grandmother but he snaps to attention if the Queen notices he is doing something wrong in public. For example, William was focusing on Prince George rather than standing upright and facing the crowd, at his grandmother's 90th birthday celebrations. William received a firm tap on the shoulder from the Queen, she then gestured and mouthed at him to stand up. He did so immediately, and to add insult to injury Prince George seemed to perform a comical face palm. The video of this went viral, was shared on social media with much amusement and retweeted thousands of times. For all her reprimands, however, you could see her pride when she went to William's base at RAF Valley, shortly before his wedding. In return, he seemed delighted to show her around his yellow helicopter.

A COOL GRANNY

The Queen is immensely proud of all her grandchildren, especially the Princess Royal's daughter Zara, who shares her love of horses. Even at the age of 85, the Queen was pictured on horseback with two of her other grandchildren, Lady Louise Windsor and her brother James. All three were enjoying a gentle ride, proof that the Queen can be a rather cool granny.

The Queen reprimands Prince William during her 90th birthday celebrations, June 2016. (PA Images)

'ANNUS HORRIBILIS'

1992 was a year when the Queen experienced one of the most difficult periods of her reign. It saw the break-up of three family marriages – the separations of Prince Charles and Diana as well as the Duke and Duchess of York, and the divorce of Princess Anne and Captain Mark Phillips. In November fire swept through Windsor Castle, destroying some of the historic parts of the building. During the chaos, the Queen and the Duke of York helped rescue works of art, while 200 firefighters fought the flames.

The Queen rarely expresses personal feelings in public, but in such an unhappy year, she made an exception. In her Christmas message, she said, '1992 is not a year that I will look back on with undiluted pleasure. In the words of one of my more sympathetic correspondents, it has turned out to be an "Annus Horribilis"' The Queen also described 2019 as a 'bumpy' year, with commentators calling it her second annus horribilis

STAYING IN TOUCH

John Samson, aged 12, presents the Queen with a tablet computer by during her visit to the Royal Commonwealth Society in London, November 2012. (PA Images).

The Queen online

The Queen first sent an email in 1976 – the first monarch to do so – and posted her first tweet on 24 October 2014 while opening an information technology gallery at the Science Museum in London. It went out at 11.35am to the then 724,000 followers of the @BritishMonarchy and read: 'It is a pleasure to open the Information Age exhibition today at the @ScienceMuseum and I hope people will enjoy visiting. Elizabeth R.' It was retweeted 36,000 times and favourited 37,000 times. However, not everyone was thrilled with her foray into the social media world and her tweet received a number of foul-mouthed responses, which were later deleted. The Queen made her first Instagram post in 2019.

Royals and languages

Many members of the royal family speak at least one foreign language:

- 👑 Most of the senior royals speak some French. For example, Prince William gave a speech in Quebec entirely in French in 2011. He also speaks a little Swahili, having taught himself, and delivered a speech in the language while on a royal tour of Tanzania.
- 👑 According to reports, Prince Philip grew up in a household that spoke English, French and German.
- 👑 Learning Welsh is a big part of training to become Prince of Wales. Ahead of his official crowning, Prince Charles learned Welsh at the University College of Wales in Aberystwyth.
- 👑 Prince George and Princess Charlotte are already learning their first foreign language: Spanish.
- 👑 Prince Michael of Kent and his wife, Princess Michael, both speak Russian.

The Palace has made a conscious effort to keep abreast of modern technology and social media. It has its own website, Facebook page, and Instagram, Twitter and Flickr accounts. These modern communication tools allow the monarchy to reach out to the younger generation, not just in the UK but also throughout the Commonwealth and wider world. They all contribute to keeping the monarchy relevant.

The younger royals – William, Kate, Harry and Meghan – have hugely popular social media platforms with millions of followers. When they write, they tweet as themselves, not as a member of their communications staff, and they usually sign off with the initial of their first name. Princess Eugenie was the first royal to have an Instagram account, and is planning her own podcast.

OFFICIAL SOCIAL MEDIA ACCOUNTS RUNS BY THE ROYAL FAMILY

General
twitter: @RoyalFamily (4.05 million followers)
Facebook: @ TheBritishMonarchy (5 million followers)
instagram: @TheRoyalFamily (6.5 million followers)

Prince Harry and Meghan
instagram: @SussexRoyal (10.7 million followers)
Prince William and Kate
instagram @KensingtonRoyal (9.2 million followers)
twitter: @KensingtonRoyal (1.8 million followers)

Prince Charles and Camilla
instagtam @ClarenceHouse (863,000 followers)
twitter: @ClarenceHouse (840,600 followers)

Princess Beatrice
twitter: @YorkieBea (102,500 followers)
Princess Eugenie
instagram:@PrincessEugenie (1 million followers)

Prince William, Prince Charles and Prince Harry looking at a mobile phone during day two of the Invictus Games Athletics competition, at Lee Valley Athletics Centre, September 2014. (PA Images)

Students wait with their phones at the ready to photograph the arrival of the Prince Harry and the Duchess of Sussex at Macarthur Girls High School in Sydney on the fourth day of their visit to Australia, October 2018. (PA Images)

ROYAL DOGS

The Queen is well known for her love of dogs, and Welsh Corgis have become an internationally recognised symbol of her reign. This follows a long tradition of the royal family keeping dogs.

Among the Queen's canine-loving predecessors was Queen Victoria, who liked and kept a number of different breeds, including Dachshunds, Border Collies and Pugs. King Edward VII was fond of terriers, especially a pair called Jack and Caesar. King George V continued the tradition of keeping terriers, but also took an interest in working Labradors. The Duke of York, later King George VI, was the first to introduce Pembroke Welsh Corgis to the royal family, when he acquired two for his daughters, Elizabeth and Margaret. The Queen has kept Corgis ever since. The most famous of these was Susan – an 18th birthday present, from whom all subsequent royal Corgis are descended.

The Queen sitting on a grassy bank with the corgis at Virginia Water to watch competitors, including Prince Philip, in the Marathon of the European Driving Championship, part of the Royal Windsor Horse Show in 1973. (PA Images)

Good pedigree

The royal family are established dog breeders. In the 1840s, the royal kennels were built in Windsor Home Park large enough to house 100 dogs. Among the many dogs that have passed through are diplomatic

gifts, such as Looty, a Pekingese that was presented to Queen Victoria after the end of Second Opium War. Later that century, Queen Victoria showed six of her Pomeranians in the very first Crufts dog show in 1891. Breeding programmes of various types of dog continued at Windsor then Sandringham during the 19th and 20th centuries, and today the Queen is one of the longest-established breeders of Pembroke Corgis in the world.

Passionate about animal welfare

The royal family have long been interested in animal welfare and stopping cruel practices such as tail docking and ear cropping, which Queen Victoria banned. Victoria also gave her patronage to the Royal Society for the Prevention of Cruelty to Animals (RSPCA) and in 1885 became royal patron of Battersea Dogs and Cats Home. The Duchess of Cornwall is its current patron.

Corgis

The Queen has owned 30 Pembroke Welsh Corgis over the years, and they have been portrayed in many ways, from statues to works of art. Dookie and another Corgi called Jane were the first of these, acquired in 1933 for the two princesses. Dookie, officially named Rozavel Golden Eagle, acquired his nickname when he was sent away to be trained. The staff, aware that the dog was destined for the household of the Duke of York, began to refer to him as 'Dookie'. When the dog returned to his

Did you know?

Over the years, the Queen has owned an elephant, two giant turtles, a jaguar and a pair of sloths. All of these were presents from other countries, and all of them went to live in London Zoo.

new family it became clear that he only responded to his new nickname, so it stayed with him.

Dookie and Jane were followed by Susan. In April 2018, the last dog from Susan's lineage, Willow, passed away. The Queen has now stopped breeding Corgis because she does not want to leave any behind when she dies. While the loss of Willow certainly feels like the end of an era, the Queen isn't without pets. She has two dogs, Vulcan and Candy, who are part of a crossbreed created when a dachshund belonging to Princess Margaret mated with one of the Queen's Corgis.

Jack Russells

Charles and Camilla's favourite breed of dog is the Jack Russell. Charles' favourite, Tigga, was given to him as a puppy by Lady Salisbury, and was rarely away from his side during its lifetime. Following Tigga's death in 2002, the Prince was said to be 'very sad and upset'. Tigga had been prominent during key moments in the Prince's life, featuring in his 40th birthday photographs taken of the Prince, and on many Christmas cards, including the lighthearted 'Flowerpot Men' card of 1995 in which Prince William, then 13, and an 11-year-old Prince Harry were pictured popping out of giant urns.

Tigga first came to national prominence in April 1994 when his daughter, Pooh – they were both named after A.A. Milne characters – disappeared at Balmoral, leading to the biggest dog-hunt in the nation's history. The Prince, Tigga and Pooh were walking in Ballochbuie Forest on the vast Balmoral estate, when Pooh ran off. She was never seen again, despite ghillies, bailiffs and estate workers scouring the estate, and psychics offering their intuitions. The incident emerged when Charles placed a small advertisement offering a reward in a local paper. The Duke and Duchess of Cornwall currently have two Jack Russells, Bluebell and Beth, which they adopted from the Battersea Dogs and Cats Home.

Cocker spaniels

William and Catherine's pet dog Lupo, a working English Cocker Spaniel, was bred from Ella, a bitch owned by Kate's parents Michael and Carole Middleton. William decided to get the dog in 2012, to keep Kate company while he was away serving in the RAF in the Falklands Islands. Lupo – Italian for 'wolf' – also starred in the palace's first official pictures of William and Kate with baby Prince George.

Labrador-German-Shepherd mix

Meghan, the Duchess of Sussex has been a dog lover for years. Before meeting Prince Harry she adopted two

dogs – Bogart (a Labrador-German Shepherd mix) and Guy (a Beagle). However, when Meghan moved to the UK she was only able to bring Guy along; Bogart was reportedly too old to adjust to such a big move, so she left him in the care of close friends. In August 2018 it emerged that the couple welcomed a black Labrador retriever, named Oz, in to their household.

The Duchess of Sussex meets a Jack Russell called Minnie during a visit to Mayhew, an animal welfare charity, at its offices in north-west London. (PA Images)

DOGS IN ART

Favourite royal pets, especially dogs, are depicted in many works of art in the Royal Collection. For instance, in the 17th century Charles I, who made popular the King Charles spaniel, made sure that several of the dogs featured in court portraits by Sir Anthony van Dyck.

It was Queen Victoria and Prince Albert, however, who first documented their large collection of domestic dogs, commissioning Sir Edwin Landseer to paint their favourite pets. These included Dash, the spaniel that was Queen Victoria's childhood companion, and Eos, the greyhound that accompanied Prince Albert from Germany. Landseer also incorporated a number of their pets into his acclaimed painting, 'Windsor Castle in Modern Times'.

In 1854 Queen Victoria commissioned William Bambridge to photograph portraits of the dogs in the Windsor kennels, a project that continued until the Queen's death. These formal portraits continued to be commissioned after Victoria's reign, though in more recent times the most compelling photographs of royal pets are those that have been taken by their owners.

ALL THINGS EQUESTRIAN

Two Windsor Greys are readied at the Royal Mews at Buckingham Palace in preparation for pulling the carriage at the wedding of Prince Harry and Meghan Markle. (PA Images)

Like any true enthusiast, the Queen's love of horses has not dimmed over the years. Whenever the subject of horses and racing are introduced in conversation, her eyes light up. Indeed, she is said to start her day surveying the pages of the *Racing Post* – the bible of the racing fraternity, and when she was overseas, it was faxed to her.

The Queen's parents encouraged this love of horses. Both were keen racehorse-owners and breeders. In 1942, when she was 16, Princess Elizabeth was taken to the royal stables at Beckhampton in Wiltshire, where she stroked her father's then unbeaten racehorse Big Game. She was said to have been so excited that she did not wash her hands for several hours afterwards. Her own first racehorse, the filly Astrakhan, was a wedding present from the Aga Khan in 1947. Since then, the Queen has owned and bred scores of thoroughbreds. She now has around 25 horses in training most years, most of them bred from the royal studs.

Champion owner

The Queen's interest in racing developed after she inherited her father's racehorses in 1952. In the 1950s, she enjoyed great success, including winning two of British horse racing's five 'classic' flat races: the Oaks at Epsom in 1957 and the 2,000 Guineas at Newmarket in 1958. She was so successful that in 1954 and again in 1957, she was named British flat racing's Champion

Owner – the title being awarded to the owner whose horses have won the most prize money that season. Another successful year for her was 1977, her Silver Jubilee year, when Dunfermline was victorious at the Oaks at Epsom and the St Leger Stakes at Doncaster.

There is, however, one race that has so far eluded her: the Derby Stakes at Epsom, which is the most prestigious of the five classic flat races. It is still her ambition, and that of her racing team, to win this race. But she has never done better at the Derby than in 1953, when Aureole finished second. Her most recent try was in 2011 when Carlton House finished third after losing a shoe close to the finishing line.

Royal Ascot

Royal Ascot, also in June, is another important fixture in the Queen's year. She first attended in 1945, and has been going ever since. In earlier years, one of her favourite pastimes was to canter down the course in the early morning.

The Queen has for many years hosts an annual house party at Windsor Castle during Ascot week. For four days, she, Prince Philip and her guests travel by car to the racecourse gates after lunch, where they transfer into open horse-drawn carriages for the traditional procession along the racecourse to the royal box. The Queen has had 20 winners at Royal Ascot over the years.

The Royal Windsor Horse Show

The Queen's passion for horses is not restricted to thoroughbreds and racehorses. Each May, she attends the Royal Windsor Horse Show – the largest outdoor equestrian show in the UK, which is held in what is effectively her back garden at Windsor Castle. More

Did you know?
Although she never bets on her own horses, the Queen doesn't mind a tiny sweepstake. There is always one in the royal box that day, with all the guests sticking a pound in the pot.

than 3,000 horses and ponies take part in 250 jumping, showing and carriage-driving classes.

The Queen and 'The Horse Whisperer'

Monty Roberts, the inspiration for the 1998 Hollywood film *The Horse Whisperer* has been consulting the Queen on her horses and Corgis for a quarter of a century. Renowned for his taming of wild animals, Mr Roberts, from California, regularly meets the monarch, staying at her royal estates to work with her animals and discuss all things equine. In an interview about his work with the Queen, he said, 'If she hadn't pushed me, I'd be a cowboy in California doing parochial stuff. It's always helpful when the British monarch is a fan.'

Eventing and show jumping

Princess Anne and her daughter Zara Tindall are perhaps the royal family's greatest equestrians. At the age of 21, Princess Anne won the individual title at the European Eventing Championship, and was voted the BBC Sports Personality of the Year in 1971. She was a member of the British Eventing Team, winning 2 silver medals in the 1975 European Eventing Championship, and she competed in the Olympic Games, in 1976.

In 2006, Zara followed in her mother's footsteps and won individual and team gold medals at the European Eventing Championship. The same year, she too was voted BBC Sports Personality of the Year.

Polo

Prince Philip helped make the sport of polo popular in the UK, having been taught by his uncle, Earl Mountbatten in Malta during World War II. When Prince Philip returned to England, he formed the Windsor Park team and then the Guards Polo Club. He carried on playing the sport until he was 50, when arthritis meant that he had to retire. By this time, however, Philip had passed on his passion to Charles, to whom he gave a mallet when he was 15. Charles went on to compete four years later and was once quoted as saying that it was his 'one great extravagance', to which he dedicated a large part of his adult life. After numerous injuries, however, in 2015 he retired to the sidelines as an avid spectator.

Today, the tradition continues,: both William and Harry now play polo, and their young families are regular spectators. Like many social sporting events, polo has

Did you know?

Prince William is left-handed, something that was publically revealed in 1991 when he signed his name in the visitors' book at Llandaf Cathedral in Wales. This posed a handicap for the polo-playing prince, because the game permits the use of the right hand only, but he was determined to learn.

become synonymous with charity fundraisers. Together, since 2007, William and Harry have raised more than £7 million from polo events.

Carriage driving

The Duke of Edinburgh has long enjoyed the sport of four-in-hand carriage driving, which he started after he gave up playing polo at the age of 50. He went on to help construct a sporting carriage from something he called the 'Balmoral dog cart.' The Countess of Wessex and her daughter Lady Louise Windsor share Philip's passion: mother and daughter spend time together preparing to compete in the Royal Windsor Horse Show, where they have taken part in the British Driving Society Class.

The Queen and her daughter, Princess Anne, riding near Windsor Castle with a member of staff from the royal stables. March 2002. (PA Images)

SPORTING EVENTS

The Commonwealth Games

The Queen believes that sport is a great force for good and can be used to build communities and create harmony in society. Perhaps that is why she places such emphasis on supporting the Commonwealth Games, also known as the 'friendly games' – a world-class, multi-sports event that is held once every four years.

The Games were first held in London in 1911 as part of a Festival of Empire, celebrating the coronation of King George V. Known that first year as the Inter-Empire Sports Meeting, the competing countries – the UK, Canada, South Africa, Australia, New Zealand and Tasmania – took part in nine events at London's Crystal Palace. Canada was declared the winner, and presented with an 800cm (315in)-high silver trophy called the Lonsdale Cup.

Plans to stage any more games were overshadowed by the start of World War I. However, 17 years later, in 1928, Canada proposed holding the first 'British Empire Games' in Hamilton. After weeks of negotiations, which included offering free lodging and travel grants for competitors, it was announced that the Games would be held in Canada in August 1930.

The organisers produced a constitution, which read: 'It will be designed on the Olympic model, both in general construction and its stern definition of the amateur. But the games will be very different, free from both excessive stimulus and the babel of the

Retired cyclist Anna Mears from Australia carries the baton after receiving it from Queen Elizabeth II at the launch at Buckingham Palace, London of The Queen's Baton Relay for the XXI Commonwealth Games being held on the Gold Coast in 2018. (PA Images)

> ### THE NAME OF THE GAMES
>
> *The Commonwealth Games has seen various name changes over the years:*
>
> - *Between 1930 and 1950, the Games were known as the British Empire Games.*
> - *Between 1954 and 1966, they were called the British Empire and Commonwealth Games.*
> - *The word 'Empire' was dropped in 1970, when it became the British Commonwealth Games.*
> - *Finally, in 1978, the Games were given the name the Commonwealth Games, and this is how they are known today.*

international stadium. They should be merrier and less stern, and will substitute the stimulus of novel adventure for the pressure of international rivalry.'

In the 1930 Games, 400 athletes competed from 11 countries: Canada, Australia, England, Bermuda, Newfoundland, New Zealand, Ireland, Scotland, South Africa, Wales and British Guyana. They took part in six sports, and 59 events. It was agreed that from then on, the Games would take place every four years. They were next held at the White City Stadium in London in 1934, involving 500 athletes from 16 countries, including Hong Kong, India, Jamaica, Rhodesia and Trinidad.

The world began to notice the importance of these Games in 1954, when they featured the 'miracle mile': the first time that two runners – Roger Bannister and John Landy – ran at a pace of less than four minutes a mile in the same race. It was an historic moment.

In the 1958 Games in Cardiff, 10 world records were broken. That same year also saw demonstrations in Cardiff and London with people unhappy that South Africa's white-only team had been selected on the basis of race and colour. The country withdrew from the Commonwealth three years later, and was not readmitted until 1994, after apartheid had ended.

The Queen's Baton Relay

This Commonwealth Games tradition was first introduced at the Cardiff Games in 1958. At Buckingham Palace, the Queen handed over her Games message, enclosed in a specially designed silver-gilt baton, to two

relay runners. The baton was then carried by a team of runners to Cardiff so that the message could be read out by the Duke of Edinburgh.

The tradition still lives on, although now the message travels much longer distances. In 2006, for example, the Queen's baton visited every single Commonwealth nation and territory taking part – a total of 71 nations, on a journey of 180,250km (112,000 miles). It took a year and a day to reach its destination in Melbourne.

Today, the baton contains a tracking device so that its location can be viewed live on the Commonwealth Games' website. The 2010 baton also had text messaging capabilities so that messages of support could be sent to the baton bearers. In addition, it was embedded with lights that changed colour to reflect the flags of each country it was travelling in.

Para-sports

Para-sports were included as full medal events for the first time at any multi-sports event at the 2002 Games in Manchester. Twenty countries sent male and female athletes with a disability to compete in 10 events across five different sports: athletics, lawn bowls, swimming, table tennis and weightlifting. Since then, the number of para-events has grown and for the 2010 Delhi games athletes competed in 15 medal events.

The Invictus Games

During a visit to the USA in 2013, Prince Harry visited the 'Warrior Games', a competition for wounded servicemen organised by the US Department of Defense. He was so inspired by what he saw that he 'stole' (his words) the idea and brought it back to the UK. The next year, 2014, the first Invictus Games took place in London. Since then, Prince Harry has remained involved with Invictus, serving as patron of the Invictus Games Foundation, and has attended every Games to date. The next Games will take place in the Netherlands in 2020.

ROYAL FOOTBALL FANS

Prince William, who is president of the Football Association, loves football and regularly plays with his friends. He is an Aston Villa fan and has attended lots of matches ever since he was first taken to Villa Park as a child. In 2010, alongside David Beckham, he was part of the UK bid to host the 2018 World Cup. The Queen, meanwhile, is understood to have had a soft spot for Arsenal since meeting Arsène Wenger at an event at Buckingham Palace in 2007. Prince Harry is an Arsenal fan too. Prince Charles also likes to watch football, and was given a VIP season ticket in 2012 when he revealed he was a secret Burnley supporter.

ROYAL CHARTERS IN THE ARTS

The Queen and Prince Philip arriving at the London Palladium for the Royal Variety Performance, November 1957. (PA Images)

Above right: Prince Charles joins Darcey Bussell (centre right) on stage for the curtain call after a winter gala performance of opera and ballet at the Royal Opera House, London, in 2004. (PA Images)

A royal charter is a formal document issued by a monarch granting a right or power to an individual or a corporate body. The charters are used to establish significant organisations such as cities or universities or in the arts.

The British monarchy has so far issued nearly 1,000 royal charters since they were first granted in the 13th century. Of these, about 750 remain in existence. Among the best-known organisations established by royal charter are the BBC, the Bank of England, the British Red Cross and the British Council. Royal charters are granted by the Privy Council and are not put before Parliament.

Royal Shakespeare Company

The Royal Shakespeare Company (RSC) was established on 20 March 1961 with a royal charter and the announcement that the Shakespeare Memorial Theatre in Stratford-upon-Avon would be called the Royal Shakespeare Theatre . Prince Charles, who has long been an advocate of teaching Shakespeare in schools, has been president since 1991.

Royal Variety Performance

The Royal Variety Performance has been staged for more than 100 years, making it the longest-running entertainment show in the world. Today, it is watched by more than 152 million television viewers worldwide. Its sole patron is the Queen, although the show is synonymous with the royals in general, with many senior members of the family having attended over the years. It begins with the entrance of the members of the royal family, followed by singing of the national anthem. The show raises money for the Royal Variety Charity of which the Queen is life patron.

Royal Opera House

The Royal Opera was formed in 1946 as the Covent Garden Opera Company, although operatic performances have been given in Covent Garden on the site since 1732. The current theatre was built in 1858. When the idea of public subsidy of the arts was accepted in the post-war years, the Royal Opera House was established as the year-round home of the companies now known as the Royal Opera and the Royal Ballet.

The strong royal connection is well established, Prince Charles has been patron of the Royal Opera since 1975, president of the Friends of Covent Garden since 1978, and patron of the Royal Opera House since 2015. The Royal Ballet received its royal charter on 9 October 1956 and Charles has been its president since 2004.

FASHION AND THE ROYALS

Being part of the royal family means complying with a lot of traditions and rules, some of them unbending – especially when it comes to what to wear to public engagements. Etiquette rules cover everything from hats and gloves to military uniforms.

The royals are skilled at using how they dress when in public – the colours, their jewellery, their military uniforms – to show respect to the country they are visiting, especially when on official visits to Commonwealth realms. In recent times, Meghan also garnered a lot of praise for wearing a dress that revealed the reality of what a woman looks like straight after having a baby, rather than trying to conceal or mask it.

The Queen's designers

During the 1940s and 1950s, Sir Norman Hartnell, who designed the Queen's wedding dress and coronation robes, produced many of her finest evening dresses, using sumptuous silks and duchesse satins. Hardy Amies began designing clothes for the Queen in the early 1950s, while these days, she often wears designs by Stewart Parvin. The Queen's wardrobe encompasses all the colours of the rainbow. She is reported to have once said: 'If I wore beige, nobody would know who I am.'

The Queen's dresser

Liverpool-born fashion designer, dressmaker and milliner Angela Kelly has served as personal assistant and senior dresser to the Queen since 2002 and is responsible for the Queen's clothes, jewellery and insignia. She took over from Margaret 'Bobo' MacDonald, who served her 'little lady' for 67 years, moving from nursery maid to dresser.

The Queen sits next to Anna Wintour (right) as they view Richard Quinn's catwalk show before presenting him with the inaugural Queen Elizabeth II Award for British Design in central London, February 2018. Angela Kelly, the Queen's senior dresser sits on Anna Wintour's left. (PA Images)

Kelly's role extends beyond clothes, however, and she has become as much a confidante to the Queen as an employee, with other staff members reporting they can often be heard laughing together. Kelly researches the venues for royal visits as well as the significance of different colours, in order to create appropriate outfits. She is credited for introducing the bold tones the Queen often wears while on duty to ensure members of the public see her. During Royal Ascot in particular, the Queen's taste in fashion comes under the closest

WHAT'S IN THE QUEEN'S HANDBAG?

The Queen is usually seen with her ubiquitous Launer handbag, which is probably as much associated with her as are her corgis. She may not carry money but she always has mint lozenges, reading glasses, a fountain pen, lipstick and tissues inside. She also has a portable hook stowed away in there so she can hang her bag discreetly under tables.

Angela Kelly, personnel dresser to Her Majesty wears her Royal Victorian Order medal, presented to her by the Queen at the Investiture ceremony at Buckingham Palace, November 2012. (PA Images)

Prince Charles, immaculately dressed, in suit, tie, pocket square and cufflinks, signs a visitors' book at the Royal Garden Party held at Castle Coole, Northern Ireland, May 2019. (PD CC BY 2.0)

scrutiny. Every day of the meeting, money is won and lost based on what colour hat she will be wearing.

The Queen and her gloves

Gloves, which were traditionally considered essential as well as a fashion item also have a practical purpose, helping to stop germs being spread – something that is particularly useful when you shake hands with hundreds of people every year. Despite the advantages, though, the Queen doesn't always wear gloves when meeting people – it depends on what she is wearing, where she is and what she is doing.

The Queen's hats

The Queen has become known for her bold hats, which she is often pictured wearing at official engagements, in line with tradition. Indeed, until the 1950s ladies were very seldom seen without a hat, at inside functions as well as outside, as it was not considered appropriate for them to show their hair in public.

Military style

The royals often wear military uniforms when on duty. This is because senior royals often have a number of honorary ranks as well as having served in the military, but also because uniform is especially appropriate when they represent their regiments at occasions that are military affairs, such as Trooping the Colour or services to honour British troops.

Uniform is worn on other occasions, too, especially royal weddings. Prince William, for instance, served in the RAF, but also holds the title of Colonel of the Irish Guards and he chose to represent the regiment by wearing its colours for his 2011 wedding to Catherine.

Prince Harry chose to wear the Blues and Royals military single-breasted frock-coat uniform, made of blue doeskin at his wedding. His best man, William, wore the same uniform as it is the regiment in which they both served. By doing so, the princes were following in the footsteps of their father and their grandfather: Charles wore full dress naval commander uniform when he married Lady Diana Spencer in 1981 and Philip wore his Royal Navy uniform when he married Princess Elizabeth in 1947. When Charles married his second wife, Camilla, in 2005, however, he chose not to wear a uniform, instead opting for a tailored morning suit.

Charles's snappy dressing

Always immaculately turned out, Prince Charles has twice been voted among the world's best-dressed men by *Gentlemen Quarterly*, in 2009 and in 2019. His signature look is a lightweight two-piece wool suit tailored by Royal Warrant of Appointment holders Anderson & Sheppard with a Turnbull & Asser made-to-measure shirt and silk tie, usually sporting regimental stripes, which have become bolder and brighter.

Charles's top pocket square has become more visible over the years and you can often see a flower in the buttonhole and a lapel badge. His outfits are often made in sustainable way by local craftspeople – Charles is after all a global patron of the Campaign for Wool – a cross-sector initiative to promote wool as a natural, renewable and biodegradable alternative to synthetic fibres.

Catherine's clothes

On Canada Day 2011 in Ottawa, the Duchess of Cambridge showed exactly how royals use fashion to compliment their hosts, knowing the local press will pick up on it. For the occasion, the duchess wore a cream Reiss dress and a red hat by Lock & Company's Sylvia Fletcher that appeared to feature a maple leaf, which has slowly caught on as a national symbol. In so doing, her clothes matched those of the hundreds of people who had turned out for her first overseas engagement with her husband, who were also dressed in the national colours. Kate finished off her look with a maple leaf-shaped diamond brooch, which the Queen loaned her for the tour and that had first been worn by the Queen on her visit to Canada in 1951.

On the three-week royal tour of New Zealand and Australia in 2012, Kate again reached into the Queen's jewellery box and borrowed a fern-shaped platinum and diamond brooch, which the Queen had first worn in 1954 on a Commonwealth tour. She also wore clothes by local designers and won plaudits from the press

Prince William and Catherine, on their first royal tour as a married couple, visiting Ottawa for Canada Day celebrations. In colours designed to honour her hosts, Catherine wore a cream-ruffled Reiss dress, a red Sylvia Fletcher fascinator and a diamond brooch that belongs to the Queen. (PA Images)

when she opted for a summery white eyelet frock by Zimmermann, the cool-girl Australian label.

Keeping it casual

Even when dressing casually there is still a dress code for the royals to adhere to if they are going to be seen in public. Women are expected to wear a smart day dress or trousers and a jacket or cardigan, while men generally go for a blazer with a collared shirt and chinos. Jeans, which younger royals do sometimes wear, are only appropriate for dress-down days, or for walking the dog.

Prince William and Kate, sticking closely to royal rules for informal dress, visit Auckland's Viaduct Harbour during their New Zealand tour on April 11, 2014. (Shutterstock)

CHARLES AND HIS CUFFLINKS

In 1998, Prince Charles was handed back jewellery that had been stolen four years previously by an Italian cat burglar on holiday in London. The valuables, stolen from St James's Palace, were recovered by the Italian authorities from the kitchen of Renato Rinino, 35, dubbed the 'Riviera jewel thief', in Italy. Among the items recovered were five tie pins, six gold buttons, two watches, five sets of cufflinks and two silver boxes. They included a pair of gold Fabergé cufflinks once owned by the last Tsar of Russia, which had been presented to the Prince as a christening gift. Charles celebrated in public by wearing one of the five sets of cufflinks from the haul within hours of the handover by Scotland Yard's organised crime officers.

ROYAL WEDDING DRESSES

Perhaps the most famous, and important, royal clothes are the royal wedding dresses, which not only show off the bride's beauty but are also full of symbolism. From Princess Margaret and the Queen to Princess Diana, Meghan and Kate, all have used fashion to send signals, while also supporting British and Commonwealth designers.

The Queen's dress

VITAL STATISTICS

YEAR: *1947*
DESIGNER: *Sir Norman Hartnell*
COUTURE HOUSE: *Hartnell*
FABRIC: *Soft Damascus Prokar (silk, wool, linen, cotton, or synthetic fibres, with a pattern formed by weaving)*
EMBELLISHMENT: *Crystals and 10,000 seed pearls*
TRAIN: *3.96m (13ft)*
ESTIMATED COST: *The dress was purchased using ration coupons*

After World War II, when Princess Elizabeth planned to marry Prince Philip, rationing was still being imposed. Keen to continue to shoulder her responsibilities, Elizabeth saved her rationing coupons to buy the essential materials for the dress, helped along by a gift of 200 coupons from the government. (She had to return the many hundreds of coupons sent in by the public, as it would have been illegal to accept them.)

Despite the unconventional funding, couturier Sir Norman Hartnell's design included ivory silk, duchesse satin, silver threads, crystals and 10,000 seed pearls, and the dress featured full-length sleeves, a fitted bodice, a heart-shaped neckline, a floor-length panelled skirt and a dramatic 4.5m (14.8ft)-long train. An article in *Harper's Bazaar* magazine said that the dress took inspiration from Renaissance painter Botticelli's *Primavera* and symbolised Britain's 'rebirth and growth'.

THE CORONATION DRESS

The Queen's coronation white satin dress, again designed by Sir Norman Hartnell, incorporated embroidery showing national and Commonwealth emblems in seed pearls, crystals, coloured silks and gold and silver thread.

Lady Diana Spencer's dress

VITAL STATISTICS

YEAR: *1981*
DESIGNER: *David and Elizabeth Emanuel*
FABRIC: *Ivory silk taffeta and antique lace gown*
EMBELLISHMENT: *10,000 pearls and thousands of sequins*
TRAIN: *7.62m (25ft) taffeta train and a 140m (153 yard) tulle veil*
ESTIMATED COST: *£151,000*

Perhaps the most famous royal wedding dress of the modern era, Diana's ivory silk taffeta and lace antique gown had a 7.6m (25ft)-long train and was valued at £151,000 in 1981. Designed by husband-and-wife team David and Elizabeth Emmanuel, the dress was embroidered with thousands of sequins and more than 10,000 pearls. In addition to being the most secretive design project of its time, the Emmanuels were challenged by practical issues posed by both the dress and the bride, who lost a lot of weight before the wedding. The silk of the dress and the train was prone to creasing and en route to St Paul's Cathedral, despite Diana's best efforts, the smooth finish couldn't be preserved. Nevertheless, the dress certainly had the wow factor, and remains an icon to this day.

Diana, Princess of Wales, wearing an Emanuel wedding dress, and Prince Charles, Prince of Wales leave St. Paul's Cathedral following their wedding on 29 July 1981. (PA Images)

Camilla Parker-Bowles's dresses

VITAL STATISTICS

Dress 1: For the civil ceremony at Windsor Guildhall

YEAR: *2005*

DESIGNER: *Antonia Robinson and Anna Valentine*

COUTURE HOUSE: *Robinson Valentine*

FABRIC: *Cream silk chiffon dress*

EMBELLISHMENT: *The hem was of Swiss-made appliquéed woven discs, and Camilla wore pinned to the right lapel of her matching coat a Prince of Wales feathers brooch, which consists of diamonds and a single grey pearl*

HAT: *Cream, featuring French lace and a feather trim, by milliner Philip Treacy*

ESTIMATED COST: *not known*

Dress 2: For the service of dedication and prayer at St George's Chapel

YEAR: *2005*

DESIGNER: *Antonia Robinson and Anna Valentine*

COUTURE HOUSE: *Robinson Valentine*

FABRIC: *Embroidered pale blue and gold damask dress coat with gold embroidery around the collar over a matching chiffon floor-length dress*

HAT: *Gold leaf feather headdress, tipped with Swarovski diamonds, by Philip Treacy*

ESTIMATED COST: *Not known*

The Clarence House official photo of the Prince of Wales and his new bride Camilla, Duchess of Cornwall, wearing dress number two, in the White Drawing Room at Windsor Castle. (Hugo Burnand/PA Images)

Camilla wore two outfits on the big day: a loose-fitting white knee-length dress under a basketweave coat for the civil service, then a soft, pale blue chiffon dress worn under a gold damask coat for the blessing at St George's chapel. Both outfits were designed by Antonia Robinson and Anna Valentine and were topped off by creations by Camilla's favourite milliner, Philip Treacy.

The striking headpiece worn with the second outfit was crafted from hand-dyed golden feathers that highlighted the golden embroidery detail on the damask coat. Camilla rewore her first wedding dress in 2007, when she attended the opening of the National Assembly of Wales.

The formal wedding ceremony of Charles and Camilla took place at Windsor Guildhall and was followed a 'Service of Prayer and Dedication' at St George's Chapel, conducted by the Archbishop of Canterbury.

Catherine Middleton's dress

VITAL STATISTICS

YEAR: *2011*
DESIGNER: *Sarah Burton*
COUTURE HOUSE: *Alexander McQueen*
FABRIC: *English and Chantilly lace and ivory and white satin gazar (semi-sheer) fabric*
EMBELLISHMENT: *The lace was crafted at the Royal School of Needlework, and the back of the dress was held together by 58 organza-covered buttons and rouleau loops*
TRAIN: *2.7m (8.85ft)*
VEIL: *Created at the Royal School of Needlework and crafted with hand-embroidered flowers and held in place by a Cartier halo tiara, which the Queen lent to her*
ESTIMATED COST: *£250,000*

Meghan, now Duchess of Sussex, walks down the steps of St George's Chapel with Prince Harry, after their wedding in Windsor Castle. (PA Images)

Kate Middleton's bridal gown was designed by Sarah Burton, the creative director of Alexander McQueen, and cost an estimated £250,000. The brand Alexander McQueen was owned by Paris-based luxury goods company Kering. This meant it was the first time a royal wedding dress hadn't been made by a British-owned fashion house. It was, however, embroidered in the UK using skilled needleworkers, who were unaware of whom the dress was for. The design incorporated lace sourced from France and England, some of which was the same design that had been used on Grace Kelly's wedding dress in 1956. The design is credited with changing wedding fashions and in this case bringing long sleeves back into vogue.

Meghan Markle's dress

VITAL STATISTICS

YEAR: *2018*
DESIGNER: *Clare Waight Keller*
COUTURE HOUSE: *Givenchy*
FABRIC: *Silk*
EMBELLISHMENT: *Embroidered flowers on the veil*
TRAIN: *5m (16.4ft)*
VEIL: *The veil was held in place by a diamond and platinum tiara*
ESTIMATED COST: *No price has been publicly released but it was estimated at £400,000*

Kate Middleton arrives at Westminster Abbey, London, before her marriage to Prince William. (PA Images)

Meghan hired British-born designer Clare Waight Keller, director of haute couture at Givenchy, to create her wedding gown using contemporary fabrics. The result was a smooth double-bonded silk gown that gave a sculptural effect in the bright sunlight, with the seams virtually invisible. Her veil was embroidered with 53 flowers, representing the Commonwealth nations.

CROWNS AND CORONETS

The Crown Jewels

The Crown Jewels represent the passing of authority from one king or queen regnant to another during the sacred coronation ceremony. The Queen herself does not personally own the jewels. The national treasures have been kept in the Jewel House, a high-security vault in the Waterloo Block (formerly a barracks) at the Tower of London.

The current Crown Jewels date back to 1661 and are based on the 11th-century originals destroyed by Parliamentarians after Charles I was executed in 1649, at the end of the Civil War. After the Interregnum, in order to regain continuity with the monarchal system, a coronation crown and a state crown, an orb, sceptre, swords, spurs, ring and bracelets were remade by Sir Robert Vyner, 1st Baronet (1621–88), a goldsmith-banker and Lord Mayor of the City of London. Charles II personally directed discussions concerning the remaking of the regalia.

ST EDWARD'S CROWN

VITAL STATISTICS
YEAR CREATED: *1661*
MATERIAL: *2-carat gold*
NOTABLE STONES: *444 precious and semi-precious stones*
CAP: *Purple velvet trimmed with ermine*
ARCHES: *2, Baroque*
WEIGHT: *2.23kg (4.9lb)*
SIZE: *30cm (12in) tall*
ESTIMATED VALUE: *£31 million*

This solid gold crown is the most sacred of all crowns, and is only used at the moment of crowning itself during a coronation ceremony. It was created in 1661 and was first used for the coronation of Charles II. From 1661 until 1911, the gemstones were hired for each coronation, and it wasn't until the coronation of George V that it was permanently set with semi-precious stones.

THE IMPERIAL STATE CROWN

VITAL STATISTICS
YEAR CREATED: *1937 (it is a replica of the crown made for Queen Victoria in 1838 by Rundell, Bridge and Rundell, then the Crown Jewellers)*
MATERIAL: *Gold, platinum, silver, velvet, ermine, 2,868 diamonds, 11 emeralds, 17 sapphires, spinel, 269 pearls, 4 rubies*
NOTABLE STONES: *The Lesser Star of Africa (Cullinan II), set in the front band, the Stuart Sapphire, St Edward's Sapphire, the Black Prince's Ruby and four pendant pearls, of which two may have been among the seven that Catherine de' Medici gave to Mary, Queen of Scots and which subsequently belonged to Elizabeth I*
CAP: *Velvet trimmed with ermine*
WEIGHT: *1.06kg (2.3lb)*
SIZE: *31.5cm (12.4in)*
ESTIMATED VALUE: *There is no official record of how much the Imperial State Crown is worth, but the collection has an estimated value of £3–£5 billion; the Cullinan I diamond, which is the largest gem in the collection, is said to be worth £400 million alone*

The Imperial State Crown is usually worn by the monarch for the State Opening of Parliament and other

Above left: St Edward's Crown on display during a service to celebrate the 60th anniversary of the Coronation of Queen Elizabeth II at Westminster Abbey, London. (PA Images)

Above: The Imperial State Crown is carried on a cushion as it arrives for the State Opening of Parliament, at the Houses of Parliament in London. (PA Images)

The crown of Queen Elizabeth the Queen Mother lies on her coffin as it passes into Whitehall during the ceremonial procession, when it travelled from the Queen's Chapel at St James's Palace to Westminster Hall. The Queen Mother wore the crown during the coronation of her husband, the late King George VI. (PA Images)

formal occasions. It is also the crown that the monarch wears as they leave Westminster Abbey at the end of the coronation ceremony.

Created in 1937, the crown is one of the newer items in the regalia, but it contains some of the most historic jewels in the collection. These include the 'Black Prince's Ruby' in the cross at the front of the crown. This is misnamed as it is actually a balas or spinel, a semi-precious stone. Legend says it was given to Edward, (the Black Prince) in 1367 by Pedro the Cruel, King of Castile.

Queen Elizabeth, The Queen Mother's Crown

VITAL STATISTICS
YEAR CREATED: *1937*
MATERIAL: *Platinum, diamonds, rock crystal, velvet, ermine*
NOTABLE STONES: *2,800 diamonds, including the infamous 105-carat Koh-i-Nûr*
CAP: *Purple velvet trimmed with ermine*
WEIGHT: *Not known*
SIZE: *20.7cm (8.15in)*
ESTIMATED VALUE: *Not known*

A CURSED JEWEL
The name Koh-i-Noor means 'Mountain of Light' in Persian but its history is anything but light, being marked with a succession of dark acts, provoking greed and envy. Among the things that have happened to its owners are disasters such as being blinded, poisoned, tortured, burned in oil, threatened with drowning, crowned in molten lead and battered to death. Fortunately, none of these fates befell the Queen Mother!

This crown was made in 1937 for the coronation of Elizabeth's husband George VI, using many stones already in the collection; most of the 2,800 diamonds set into its platinum frame came from Queen Victoria's Regal Circlet. The large Turkish diamond, known as the Koh-i-Noor at the front was a gift from Sultan Abdul Medjid to Victoria in 1856.

Jewelled Sword of Offering

VITAL STATISTICS
YEAR CREATED: *1821*
MATERIAL: *22-carat gold, blued and gilt steel and silver*
NOTABLE STONES: *Diamonds, rubies, emeralds*
SCABBARD: *Leather, gold, diamonds, rubies, emeralds, sapphires, turquoise*
ESTIMATED VALUE: *It cost £5,988 (about £501,400 in 2019) to make*

Not to be confused with the Sword of State, which appears at every opening of parliament, the Jewelled Sword of Offering is for coronations only. It was forged in 1821, and is presented to the new monarch during the ceremony as part of a collection of 'ornaments', which represents the chivalric nature of monarchy. The sword is fastened around the waist of kings (but not queens) before it is offered up at the altar.

Sovereign's Orb

VITAL STATISTICS
YEAR CREATED: *1661*
MATERIAL: *Gold*
NOTABLE STONES: *Emeralds, rubies, sapphires, diamonds, pearls*
SIZE: *16.5cm (6.5in)*
WEIGHT: *1.19kg (2.63lb)*
ESTIMATED VALUE: *It cost £1,150 (about £160,000 in 2019) to make in 1661*

Consisting of a hollow gold sphere, the Sovereign's Orb is mounted with clusters of emeralds, rubies and sapphires surrounded by rose-cut diamonds, and single rows of pearls. A cross on the top is set with rose-cut diamonds, with a sapphire in the centre on one side and an emerald on the other, and with pearls at the angles and at the end of each arm. It is placed in the monarch's right hand, then on the altar during the coronation.

Sceptre and rod

VITAL STATISTICS

Sovereign's Sceptre with Dove (also known as the Rod of Equity and Mercy)

YEAR CREATED: *1661*

MATERIAL: *Plain gold rod, topped by a gold globe and cross supporting an enamelled dove*

NOTABLE STONES: *Diamonds, rubies, emeralds, including the Cullinan Diamond*

SIZE: *110.2cm (43in)*

WEIGHT: *11.15kg (2.5lb)*

ESTIMATED VALUE: *Not known*

Sovereign's Sceptre with Cross

YEAR CREATED: *1661 with later additions*

MATERIAL: *Gold and enamel*

NOTABLE STONES: *Diamonds, emeralds, rubies, sapphires, spinels, amethyst*

SIZE: *92.2cm*

WEIGHT: *1150g*

ESTIMATED VALUE: *Not known*

These two items are an important part of the coronation ceremony, and are placed in each of the monarch's hands in the last part of the investiture, before the crowning itself. The significance of their predecessors was described at the coronation of William the Conqueror in 1066: 'by the sceptre uprising in the kingdom are controlled, and the rod gathers and confines those men who stray.' The rod also symbolises the monarch's pastoral care for his or her people.

The current Sovereign's Sceptre with Cross was created for the coronation of Charles II in 1661 and has been used at every coronation since. For George V's, it was transformed by the addition of the spectacular Cullinan Diamond – the largest top-quality cut white diamond in the world, weighting in at 530.2 carats. The Sovereign's Sceptre with Dove, again dating from around 1661, is topped by an enamel dove with open wings perched on a cross to symbolise the Holy Ghost.

Other coronation paraphernalia

CORONATION CHAIR

Dating from 1300, this chair was spared during the Interregnum because Cromwell wanted to use it at Westminster Hall when he was installed as Lord Protector in 1653.

THE CROWN JEWELLER

The crown jeweller is responsible for the maintenance of the Crown Jewels. The post was created by Queen Victoria in 1843, when she issued a royal warrant to Garrard & Co and the title of crown jeweller was vested on an employee of the company. Only the crown jeweller is authorised to handle the Crown Jewels; others may only do so with his or her permission. In 2008 Harry Collins, of Tunbridge Wells, Kent, was appointed crown jeweller. Collins gave up the post in 2017. The current crown jeweller, the 10th, is Mark Appleby, of Mappin & Webb.

ANOINTING AMPULLA

After the coronation oath has been made, the monarch is anointed by the Archbishop of Canterbury on his or her hands, breast and head. The oil is poured from the Ampulla – a golden eagle-shaped flask that dates from 1661 – into the Coronation Spoon.

CORONATION SPOON

Dating from 1349, the spoon is the only part of the mediaeval Crown Jewels collection that survived the Commonwealth of England destruction. It is made from silver gilt and features an oval bowl that is divided into two lobes and engraved. Between the bowl and the stem are two stylised monster's heads, positioned either side of a roundel that is set with four pearls.

Queen Elizabeth II wearing the Imperial State Crown and holding the orb and sceptre, after her coronation in Westminster Abbey. (PA Images)

STATE OCCASIONS
AND OFFICIAL
ENGAGEMENTS

CORONATIONS

The Archbishop of Canterbury, Geoffrey Francis Fisher, places the Crown of St Edward on the head of the Duke of York, thus making him King George VI, 12 May 1937. (PA Images)

The first account of a coronation ceremony dates back to 973AD when King Edgar was crowned in Bath. Since then, although the location moved to London in 1066, the rituals involved with the passing of authority from one monarch to another have changed little, and the ceremony today is still composed of a number of traditional elements.

The processions

In the days before mass media, or even television and radio, the processions that took place before and after the coronation ceremony provided a means for many thousands of people to see and feel involved in the occasion. What's more, the ceremony and spectacle were also intended as ways to gain popular support for the new monarch – a tradition that started in 1377 when 10-year-old Richard II rode at the head of a great procession of dignitaries and nobles through the streets of London, where bands played, wine flowed, banners flew and the wealth of the king was on show in the form of a dazzling display of gold, silver and jewels.

Following on from this event, the procession for more than 300 years followed a route from the Tower of London to Westminster Abbey, where crowds would gather outside while the ceremony took place inside. Since Victoria's coronation in 1838, however, the procession starts and ends at Buckingham Palace.

The oath

Once the new monarch has arrived at the Abbey and taken his or her seat on a Chair of Estate, the coronation can begin. First comes the Recognition, when the assembled congregation (representing the people) take it in turn on all four sides – north, south, east and west – to shout their acceptance of the monarch. In response, the monarch pledges an oath before God to rule fairly and to protect the church. They may also make an Accession Declaration, in which they swear to be faithful to the Protestant faith. A Bible is then placed in the monarch's hands and Holy Communion begins.

The anointing

Shortly after it begins, the Holy Communion service is interrupted and an anthem is played as the prelude to

Men of the Royal Horse Guards who will form part of the Sovereign's Escort at the Coronation checking the ceremonial full dress equipment, which they will be wearing. Corporal of Horse J. Hammond, left, receives his uniform from Corporal of Horse J. Peart at Knightsbridge Barracks. (PA Images)

Far right: the Royal Navy detachment passes Nelson's Column in Trafalgar Square on the march from Westminster Abbey to Buckingham Palace after the coronation of Queen Elizabeth II. (PA Images)

the next phase of the process – the anointing. Prayers and a further anthem – 'Zadok the Priest' – come next, during which the monarch removes one robe, moves to the Coronation Chair, and dons the anointing gown. Once the monarch is seated, a canopy of golden cloth, borne aloft by four Knights of the Garter, is placed over the monarch's head in order to conceal this very private and sacred part of the ceremony from public gaze. In keeping with this, no photographs or filming of this part of the ceremony are allowed. Finally, the Dean of Westminster pours some aromatic holy oil from the Ampulla into the Coronation Spoon and passes it to the Archbishop of Canterbury, who then anoints the monarch on the hands, chest and head.

The investiture

The next stage of proceedings involves the monarch being dressed in a number of coronation robes in between receiving a series of ornaments that symbolise the chivalric nature of kingship. These include spurs, which represent chivalry, bracelets, and the Sword of Offering. Once fully robed, the archbishop presents the monarch with Sovereign's Orb, which represents the rule of Jesus over the world, before this and the Sword of Offering are placed on the altar. The last part of the investiture involves placing a ring, representing the sovereign's marriage to the nation, on the fourth finger of the right hand. They also receive the rod and sceptre.

The crowning

Finally, the climax of the ceremony arrives: the moment when the archbishop places the St Edward's Crown on the monarch's head, whereupon the congregation cries out in unison three times 'God save the King/ Queen'. Peers of the realm and officers of arms don their coronets, signalling trumpets to sound a fanfare in the Abbey, bells to ring out across the land and 62-gun salutes to boom from the Tower of London and Hyde Park. A final prayer completes the crowning.

The enthroning and homage

At this point, the monarch is guided to a raised throne, where he or she receives the oath of allegiance from the clergy and then the nobles in the Act of Homage. If there is a consort, he or she is now anointed, invested, crowned and enthroned in a rather more low-key fashion. This done, the communion service that had been interrupted earlier is concluded, after which the new monarch exchanges the coronation crown for the Imperial State Crown, and processes from the Abbey.

Queen Elizabeth II of England in full regalia after her coronation at Westminster Abbey, 2 June 1953. (Alamy)

A typical street party to celebrate the coronation in Swinbrooke Road, Kensington, attended by 253 children. The party included a bus tour of the coronation route, a show with conjurers and clowns, and a tea which included a 60lb cake. Maureen Atkins, aged 14, seen centre with her attendants, was crowned queen for the day by Father Douglas Lott, Vicar of St Michael and All Angels. (PA Images)

STATE OPENING OF PARLIAMENT

The Queen and the Duke of Edinburgh, with Prince Charles and the Duchess of Cornwall to the Queen's right, in the House of Lords, during the State Opening of Parliament, May 2015. (PA Images)

The State Opening of Parliament is the main ceremonial event of the parliamentary calendar, and involves traditions that date back to the 16th century. The only regular occasion when the three constituent parts of Parliament – the sovereign, the House of Lords and the House of Commons – meet, it takes place on the first day of a new parliamentary session or shortly after a general election and marks the official start of the parliamentary year.

Order of events

The day before the State Opening, a full dress rehearsal takes place, usually in the early hours of the morning. On the day itself, the Queen and, latterly, Prince Charles travel in procession in a state coach from Buckingham Palace to the Palace of Westminster, escorted by the Household Cavalry and with the Imperial State Crown and regalia travelling in its own carriage ahead of the Queen's coach.

The Queen and her retinue arrive at the Sovereign's Entrance at Westminster, from where she proceeds to the Robing Room and puts on the Imperial State Crown and the Robe of State. Once attired, she leads the royal procession through the usually crowded Royal Gallery to the chamber of the House of Lords, where she takes a seat on a richly gilded throne.

From here, an official known as Black Rod is sent to the Commons chamber to summon the members of Parliament, but the chamber door is shut in his face. It is often said that this practice dates back to the English Civil War, and symbolises the Commons' independence from the monarchy, but Speakers of the House have ruled that the custom is to allow the Commons to establish Black Rod's identity rather than the House asserting its right to deny him entry. Whatever the truth, Black Rod does strike the door three times with his ebony staff and it is then opened. Members of the House of Commons then file out and follow Black Rod and the Commons Speaker to the Lords' chamber to congregate in front of the Queen, standing at the opposite end of the chamber, known as the Bar of the House, to listen to the Queen's Speech.

THE QUEEN'S SPEECH

The Queen's Speech is delivered to both houses by the Queen, although it is actually written by the government, and serves to set out their agenda for the coming session, as well as outlining proposed policies and legislation. It is brought to the Queen in a silk purse by the Lord Chancellor, who presents it to her on bended knee.

AFTER THE QUEEN'S SPEECH

Having read out the speech, the Queen and her party leave the way they came. A new parliamentary session officially starts and public business is resumed as members of both the House of Lords and the House of Commons debate the content of the speech over several days, looking at various aspects of the planned legislative programme, before agreeing an 'Address in Reply to Her Majesty's Gracious Speech'. The Queen's Speech is voted on in the House of Commons.

HISTORY OF THE STATE OPENING

Some traditions surrounding the State Opening of Parliament and the delivery of a speech by the monarch can be traced back as far as the 16th century. These include the Yeomen of the Guard – the royal bodyguards – searching the cellars the evening before the ceremony, in a ritual that dates back to the 1605 Guy Fawkes gunpowder plot. Another tradition involves Buckingham Palace taking an MP – usually a junior whip – 'hostage', releasing him or her only when the Queen returns safely to the palace. This practice was introduced by Charles I, whose tempestuous relationship with Parliament ended with his beheading in 1649.

INVESTITURES

An investiture is the name for the occasion when someone receives an award from the Queen or another member of the royal family at a royal residence, usually Buckingham Palace, or else Windsor Castle or the Palace of Holyroodhouse. Investitures may also take place abroad when a senior member of the royal family permitted to carry out the function is on a state visit. A list of honours is published twice a year by the Cabinet Office: the New Year Honours, and the Birthday Honours in June. These are presented at around 30 investitures throughout the year.

The people who receive the honours, or 'gongs', are usually people who have had major achievements

INVESTITURE OF PRINCE CHARLES AS THE PRINCE OF WALES

The Queen installed her 20-year-old son Prince Charles as the Prince of Wales on 1 July 1969 at Caernarfon Castle in front of 4,000 guests. The Queen had created her eldest son Prince of Wales when he was nine years old, letting it be known that the investiture would be held when the Prince would be old enough to fully understand its significance. A TV audience of 500 million tuned in worldwide to watch the display of pomp and pageantry, with 19 million watching in the UK.

Prince Charles places his hands between those of the Queen and pays homage for the principality of Wales after his investiture at Caernarfon Castle July 1969. (PA Images)

Actress Phyllida Law wears her OBE (Officer of the Order of the British Empire) award, with daughters Sophie Thompson (l) and Emma Thompson (r)after the Investiture ceremony at Buckingham Palace, November 2014. (PA Images)

in public life, and/or committed themselves to serving Great Britain. Accomplishments range from being outstanding in a particular field to making life better for other people. There are various types of honour, depending on the field in which a person has contributed and how they have excelled. There is a limit how many honours can be awarded every year.

What happens at an investiture

The Queen or other senior member of the royal family enters the room where the investiture is taking place attended by the Queen's Body Guard of the Yeomen of the Guard and accompanied by the national anthem, which is played by the military band or orchestra.

While the band continues to play different pieces of music in the background, the recipients of the gongs are then called forwards one at a time, usually by the Lord Chamberlain, to receive their decoration and some words of congratulation from the officiating royal. If the investee is receiving a knighthood, they kneel on an investiture stool before the Queen to be dubbed with a sword. The one the Queen uses belonged to her father.

All of the planning, including the organisation of the insignia being awarded, is the responsibility of the Central Chancery of the Orders of Knighthood, a branch of the Lord Chamberlain's Office.

Did you know?

The word 'investiture' itself comes from the Latin words for dressing or robing – vestire and vestis – and refers to the formal dress that might be worn by the investee, as part of the insignia for that role.

TYPES OF HONOUR

There are six different Orders of Chivalry and two Orders of Merit into which people might be invested at various levels, known as ranks. Members of the Forces and Emergency Services may receive awards for gallantry and distinguished service.

Companion of Honour

The Order of the Companion of Honour was founded in 1917 and recognises people who have made a major contribution to the arts, science, medicine or government over a prolonged period of time. Only 65 people can hold the honour at any one time. This type of honour differs from and supercedes most of the others, which are in the Order of the British Empire.

Knight or Dame (Kt/DBE)

This premier rank of the Order of the British Empire is awarded to those who have made

a significant and inspirational contribution in a certain field, often at national level and over a long period of time. They are nominated by peers within their specialism.

Commander of the Order of the British Empire (CBE)

The next level down, a CBE is awarded to people who have held a prominent but lesser role at national level, or have played a leading role at a regional level. CBEs are also awarded to people who have made a distinguished, innovative contribution in any area.

Officer of the Order of the British Empire (OBE)

These are awarded to people who have played a major local role in any activity, including those whose work has made them nationally famous in their field.

Member of the Order of the British Empire (MBE)

An award for an outstanding achievement or service to the community that stands out as a good example to others and has had an important long-term impact.

British Empire Medal (BEM)

An award given for dedicated and effective service in the local community, such as a prolonged charitable or voluntary activity, or innovative work over a shorter period of time that has had a significant impact.

Royal Victorian Order (RVO)

This is an internal award that the Queen gives to people who have helped her personally, such as members of the Royal Household staff or British ambassadors.

JUBILEES

The Silver Jubilee

In 1977, the Queen's Silver Jubilee – to mark 25 years on the throne – was honoured with celebrations at every level throughout the country and Commonwealth. There were some mutterings among the public about cost, but when the moment to party came, the historic anniversary aroused strong feelings of loyalty among many people and up and down the UK and across the Commonwealth, and millions took the day off work to celebrate with their own street parties.

In London, some 1 million people– many of whom had camped out overnight to get a better position – lined the streets on 6 June to watch the Queen and the royal family as they made their way to St Paul's Cathedral for a special service. The Queen, dressed in pink and accompanied by Prince Philip, led the procession in the Gold State Coach as it made its way down The Mall and through Trafalgar Square, Fleet Street and Ludgate Hill.

Inside the cathedral, 2,700 selected guests – ranging from peers of the realm to politicians and other heads of state – joined in the ceremony, which opened, as had the Queen's coronation in 1953, with Ralph Vaughan Williams's arrangement of the hymn 'All People That on Earth Do Dwell'.

> ### Did you know?
> In the same year as her Silver Jubilee, the Queen became a grandmother for the first time when Princess Anne gave birth to Peter Phillips.

After the service, the Queen attended a lunch at the Guildhall, before the procession moved on its return journey to Buckingham Palace, once more cheered on by flag-waving spectators.

Other Jubilee events included the lighting of a bonfire beacon at Windsor Castle, a boat trip down the River Thames from Greenwich to Lambeth, the opening of the Silver Jubilee Walkway around parts of London and the South Bank Jubilee Gardens, a fireworks display, and various other celebrations.

Golden Jubilee

The Queen had to cope with a double loss in early 2002. In February her sister Princess Margaret died after a period of ill-health, then in March her mother died in her sleep at the age of 101. The two women had been

Performers applaud as Prince Charles kisses his mother on stage in the gardens of Buckingham Palace after the second concert to commemorate her Golden Jubilee. (PA Images)

a tremendous source of strength to the Queen, a link to her father, part of her private support system, the ultimate discreet confidantes. Now they were gone.

It was a terrible way to start the Queen's Golden Jubilee year, but afterwards the sadness turned to joy with a warm outpouring of affection for the monarch. This was evident in June, when millions took to the streets and crowded into The Mall to catch a glimpse of the royal family. The Queen also toured Britain and the Commonwealth throughout the year. During the summer, two concerts – one pop and one classical – were held at Buckingham Palace, and televised around the world. The enduring image was the rock group Queen's lead guitarist, Brian May, playing 'God Save the Queen' from the palace rooftop.

The Diamond Jubilee

The Diamond Jubilee in 2012 was a chance after six decades of service for the Queen to look back as well as forwards, and for people to pay tribute to her many years as monarch. Events included the Thames river pageant, a concert, exhibitions at various royal properties and street parties all over the country. In addition, the Queen toured England, Scotland, Wales and Northern Ireland. Her immediate family represented her too, on high-profile overseas tours throughout the countries of the Commonwealth.

THAMES DIAMOND JUBILEE PAGEANT

People turned out in their millions over a freakishly wet and cold weekend in June 2012 to watch the Queen's Diamond Jubilee pageant. Consisting of a world-record-beating 1,000-strong flotilla of tugs, steamers, pleasure

cruisers, dragon boats and kayaks, with the Queen travelling at its heart, the 11.25km (7 mile)-long parade travelled from Wandsworth to Tower Bridge in London. Taking its part in the pageant was a squadron of small boats, each one representing a member state of the Commonwealth, and the Commonwealth Choir was among the musical performers.

Pulled by a tug, the *Belfry*, carrying the Royal Jubilee Bells, was the first vessel to pass under Tower Bridge at the finish, followed by the million-pound royal row barge *Gloriana*, led by Olympic gold medallists Sir Matthew Pinsent and Sir Steve Redgrave, rowing with 16 others. As the Queen and members of her immediate family crossed the line in the royal barge, *Spirit of Chartwell*, a 41-gun salute was fired from the Tower of London to celebrate the Queen's 60 years on the throne, and thousands of people cheered.

Next, the royal family prepared to take their places on HMS *President* to watch the rest of the flotilla making its way down the Thames. However, the Duke of Edinburgh was taken ill after the pageant and had to miss much of the planned Jubilee celebrations. He, like the Queen, had stood in the cold rain on the deck of the royal barge for the duration of the voyage, refusing to sit in one of the gilded thrones provided, and appearing to onlookers to be in great spirits, resplendent in his Royal Navy uniform. Nevertheless, at the finish, his ill health became a concern and he was taken to hospital. The Queen had to go on to a service of thanksgiving in St Paul's Cathedral without him.

DIAMOND JUBILEE CONCERT

Celebrations culminated in an appearance by the Queen on the Buckingham Palace balcony in front of huge, cheering crowds. There was also a fly-past by World War II aircraft and the Royal Air Force Red Arrows. As the party rolled on, news emerged that, on the advice of his doctors, Prince Philip would have to miss the Jubilee Concert, organised by Take That singer Gary Barlow. Fortunately, Prince Charles stepped up to the mark and left his mother visibly moved by his kind, warm and sometimes emotional speech in praise of her, which also made poignant reference to his father.

The royal barge Spirit of Chartwell *carrying the Queen and other members of the royal family passes under Lambeth Bridge during the Thames pageant, 3 June 2012. (PA Images)*

BUCKINGHAM PALACE GARDEN PARTIES

D uring the summer months, the Queen hosts three garden parties at Buckingham Palace and one at Holyroodhouse in Scotland, welcoming a total of about 30,000 carefully selected guests in all. These provide a way for the Queen to come into contact with a wide range of people who have made a positive impact in their community.

The guest list
Garden parties began in the 1860s, eventually taking the place of presentation parties attended by debutants, and evolved into a way of recognising and rewarding public service. A network of sponsors – including government departments, local government, the Armed Forces, and religious insitutions – nominate guests.

The order of events
When the big day arrives, guests start to arrive from 3pm. At 4pm the party officially begins, when the Queen, accompanied by other members of the royal family, enters the garden. Her arrival is marked by one of the two military bands present playing the national anthem, after which they continue to play a selection of music. Meanwhile, the Queen and the Duke of Edinburgh move among the guests through 'lanes', each taking a different route, and presentations are made at random. This ensures that all of the guests have an equal chance of speaking to one of the royals. The Queen then goes to the Royal Tea Tent, where she meets yet more guests. The guests themselves are free to stroll around the beautiful palace gardens and enjoy the food and drink.

Dress code
Gentlemen are expected to wear morning dress or lounge suits, while women should wear day dress, usually with a hat or fascinator. National dress and uniform can also be worn.

Special garden parties
In addition to the main garden parties, the royal family hosts an annual garden party for the Not Forgotten Association, a charity for war veterans. This is usually hosted by the organisation's patron, the Princess Royal and is sometimes attended by the Queen and other members of the family. The Queen also gives permission for additional one-off garden parties to be held. In 2006, for example, the gardens were transformed into scenes from children's books for a children's party, in honour of the Queen's 80th birthday.

Meeting the Queen and other royals
There are no obligatory codes of behaviour when meeting the Queen or a member of the royal family, but many people observe the traditional forms. Men can perform a neck bow, from the head only, while women do a small curtsey. Other people prefer simply to shake hands, which is perfectly acceptable.

On presentation to the Queen, the correct formal address is 'Your Majesty' and subsequently 'Ma'am', pronounced with a short 'a' as in 'jam'. For other members of the royal family the same rules apply, with the title used in the first instance being 'Your Royal Highness' and subsequently 'Sir'. or 'Ma'am'.

Above left: Some of the food on offer during a typical garden party at Buckingham Palace. (PA Images).

Above: The Queen chats to guests during the May 2016 garden party. (PA Images)

TROOPING THE COLOUR

A 260-year-old ceremony, Trooping the Colour is a spectacle that occurs once a year to mark the official birthday of the British sovereign. One of the highlights of the royal calendar, it features more than 1,400 parading soldiers, 200 horses and 400 musicians in an impressive display of military precision, horsemanship and fanfare. Under the Queen, it takes place at the end of June, but the date of course varies from monarch to monarch.

The order of ceremony

The process begins when members of the royal family parade on horseback and in carriages from Buckingham Palace down the Mall to Horse Guard's Parade in Whitehall, cheered on by flag-waving crowds that line the streets. The Queen herself used to ride on horseback, but now she rides in a carriage.

Upon her arrival in Horse Guard's Parade, the Queen is greeted by a royal salute and then sets about her inspection of the hundreds of troops, who are fully trained and operational soldiers wearing the iconic ceremonial uniform of red tunics and bearskin hats.

Once the military bands have performed, the regimental Colour, or flag, is processed down the ranks of soldiers, who are directed with commands by the Officer in Command of the Parade. The Foot Guards next march past the Queen, forming up behind her, so that she can travel back to Buckingham Palace at their head. Back at the palace, the Queen takes the salute again from a dais before moving to the balcony, where she is joined by other members of the royal family to watch a fly-past by the RAF. The close of the ceremony is marked by a 41-gun salute fired in Green Park.

History of Trooping the Colour

British Army regimental flags were – and still are – described as 'Colours' because they display the uniform colours and insignia worn by the soldiers of different units. Traditionally, in the days before modern communications, the main role of a regiment's Colours was to provide a rallying point on the battlefield and thereby help troops to locate their unit during the heat of battle. However, in order for troops to learn exactly what their regiment's Colours were, they had to see them regularly. The best way to achieve this was for young officers to hold the Colours high and march in between serried ranks of troops on the parade ground – 'trooping the Colour'.

It is believed that this ceremony was first performed during the reign of King Charles II (1660–85). Then, in 1748, it was decided that this parade should be used to mark the official birthday of the sovereign, though it didn't become an annual event until after George III became king in 1760.

CHANGING THE GUARD

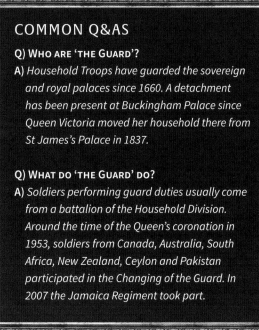

Left: Able seaman Alex Stacey (right) takes her position in a sentry box, as sailors from the Royal Navy perform the Changing of the Guard ceremony at Buckingham Palace, London, for the first time in its 357-year history, November 2017. (PA Images).

Members of the Household Cavalry at the changing The Queen's Life Guard ceremony at Horse Guards Parade January 2018. (PA Images)

Unlike Trooping the Colour, which only happens once a year, Changing the Guard – also known as Guard Mounting – happens several times a week and in two locations: outside Buckingham Palace and at Windsor Castle. Little wonder, then, that it is such a draw: it is thought that the iconic ceremony is seen by millions of people each year.

The purpose of changing the guard simply involves soldiers from the Foot Guards changing shifts. Although the soldiers work in two-hour shifts, the complete ceremony only occurs when an entire group of Foot Guards is replaced with a new one: the New Guard replacing the Old Guard. It doesn't take place every day year round, and times can vary. The weather also affects whether or not it happens, the days for each month's schedule are posted online. However, it is a regular enough spectacle to be one of the top tourist attractions in London, and the Guards certainly put on a good show as they perform the change-over, accompanied by a full military band playing a wide, sometimes surprising, range of music – from traditional marches to songs from musicals and familiar pop songs.

In addition to entertaining the crowds, however, the ceremony is of course a functional event, and it also serves as a reminder of the close relationship between the Armed Forces and the monarch.

OTHER KEY DATES FOR THE DIARY

Remembrance Day

During Remembrance Week, the Queen, Prince Charles and other members of the royal family join the nation in commemorating and honouring those who have died in the two world wars, and other conflicts, attending various engagements throughout the period. On Remembrance Sunday, the second Sunday of November, a ceremony is held at the Cenotaph, Whitehall – the focal point of the nation's homage – and the royal family, like many thousands of other people worldwide, hold a two-minute silence at 11am. After the service, a senior member of the royal family takes the Salute at the march-past of veteran organisations on Horse Guards Parade.

Swan upping

During the Middle Ages, swans were considered to be valuable commodities and were traded between noblemen. The owners of swans were duty bound to mark their property by way of a succession of unique nicks in the beaks of their birds. Any unmarked swan was owned by default by the reigning monarch. Once a mostly ceremonial occasion, the annual census of the swan population on one specific stretch of the River Thames is now an important element of wildlife conservation. Called Swan Upping, the census is carried out by swan uppers, led by the marker of the swans,

from a flotilla of traditional Thames rowing skiffs. Cygnets are ringed with identification numbers that state that the fowl belong to either the Vintners or the Dyers livery company, the only two remaining medieval organisations to own swans.

Royal Ascot

A highlight of the horse-loving Queen's calendar, Royal Ascot is special week of horse races in June that takes place at one of Britain's most well-known racecourses. In addition to the great and the good, the event is open to the general public and attracts some 300,000 visitors over the course of five days, making it Britain's most popular race meeting. Those who attend dress up in their finest clothes and hats, and the media is out in force to photograph the spectacle.

ROYAL ENCLOSURE ETIQUETTE

Men wear morning suits and top hats, while ladies are instructed to wear dresses and skirts of 'modest length' –that is those that fall just above the knee or longer. Strapless, off-the-shoulder and halter neck dresses and spaghetti straps are not permitted, though these can be covered with jackets and pashminas. The rules state that ladies should wear hats, that must have a solid base that is at least 10cm (4in) in diameter. Fascinators are not permitted.

Prince Harry and Prince William attend the annual Remembrance Sunday service at the cenotaph on Whitehall on 13 November 2016. (Getty)

The Queen's Swan uppers and the Queen's swan marker, David Barber, arrive at Henley on Thames on the third day of the swan census, July 2017. (Shutterstock)

PLAYING HOST

During her long reign, the Queen has both travelled to and hosted visitors from a huge number of different countries – more than any other British monarch. Whether playing host or guest, these visits have an important diplomatic function, serving to help strengthen Britain's relationships with countries across the world.

The visitors

The Queen does not get much of a say about whom she hosts. Instead, the Foreign and Commonwealth Office advises which foreign monarchs, presidents or prime ministers should be invited. Once this has been agreed, the incoming visits usually follow a fairly set pattern.

The welcome

Normally, the Queen and other members of the royal family greet the incoming visitors with a ceremonial welcome on Horse Guards Parade, including gun salutes. The visiting party is then invited to inspect a Guard of Honour before joining the royals in a carriage procession on the return journey to the palace, escorted by mounted soldiers from the Household Cavalry.

However, in recent times, not all state visits have started this way. For instance, in June 2019 US President Trump was helicoptered into the Buckingham Palace gardens as part of a special ceremony. Then, because

building work was being carried out at the palace, the president stayed at the US Ambassador's residence, Winfield House, near Regent's Park in central London.

The State Banquet

Having settled in, guests are normally invited to a State Banquet on the evening of their arrival. This is a very grand, formal occasion held in the Ballroom at Buckingham Palace, and involves about 150 guests, most of whom are invited on the basis of their cultural, diplomatic or economic links to the country being hosted. Once the guests have been seated and before dinner is served, the Queen traditionally makes a speech and proposes a toast to the visiting head of state, who in return replies and then proposes a toast to Her Majesty.

Behind the scenes

Away from the ball gowns and champagne, an army of staff ensures that the banquet runs smoothly. This involves a great deal of planning and preparation, often

The Queen US President, Barack Obama, pose in the music room of Buckingham Palace ahead of a State Banquet, May 2011. (PA Images)

The Queen makes a speech during the state banquet at Windsor Castle, during a two-day state visit by President Sarkozy of France and Carla Bruni-Sarkozy in 2008. (PA Images)

a year in advance of the event. The onus of responsibility lies with the Master of the Household's department – the operational arm of Buckingham Palace – and involves everything from flowers to footmen. The Queen herself is involved with the process, and checks everything is order shortly before the banquet takes place.

THE TABLE

The final build of the State Banquet table starts some five days ahead of the arrival of the visiting head of state. C-Branch, the craftsman's section of the Royal Household, has the job of assembling the 51m (168ft)-long mahogany table. It takes seven men more than three hours to build up the table leaf by leaf, then straighten it. When they have finished, the chief French polisher leaps on top, brandishing a long-handled duster. Five or six polishes later, the table is perfect.

THE TRAVELLING YEOMAN

If the state dinner is at Windsor Castle not Buckingham Palace, then the travelling yeoman's task is to ensure that the right clothes are in the right place at all times.

G-BRANCH

G-Branch – the general workers – begin tidying up in the weeks preceding the banquet. As parts of Windsor Castle are usually open to the public, there is a layer or protective Perspex lining the lower walls of all its public rooms, including the banquet hall, to stop them being scuffed. All of this has to be removed. The workaday handrails are also replaced with more elegant rails of highly polished wood.

F-BRANCH

Downstairs in the Great Kitchen – F-Branch's domain – current head chef Mark Flanagan has control of 23 chefs and nine kitchen porters and is tasked with providing a feast fit for a Queen to a large number of guests. The Queen personally chooses the main course in the five-course meal, but the rest is up to him.

To serve more than 160 people from a kitchen one floor down and hundreds of feet away, and to make sure everything remains hot, is an art in itself. It is a military-style operation involving mobile hot trolleys, jack stacks and the steady army of assistants. The hot food is transported upstairs to be laid out and garnished by chefs waiting in rooms adjoining the hall.

THE SERVERS

An under butler, a wine butler, a footman and a page are assigned to each group of nine guests. Serving begins on the green light – literally. Discreet red and green lights are stationed outside the hall doors. A series of hand signals is also used, so that for example the plate pantry yeoman can instruct an under butler to warn the palace steward, standing behind the Queen, that the food is up and ready to be served.

Like in a well-rehearsed play, each performs his or her part. Under butlers serve the food, wine butlers deliver the gravy as well as the wine, and the pages and footmen set down the plates. The honoured guest, meanwhile, enjoys his or her meal, unaware of all the frantic activity that has preceded their arrival, and will continue well into the night.

THE CLEAN-UP TEAM

By 11.30pm the banquet is over and the clearing up begins the moment the guests have left the hall. The gold dishes, gold cutlery, priceless china and engraved glasses will be swept below stairs. The washing-up, all done by hand, will be left, however, for the morning. Soon the huge kitchens will be ready for the next day, whether its a huge party of guests or just the family.

MENU FOR THE STATE BANQUET FOR BARAK AND MICHELLE OBAMA

Paupiette de Sole et Cresson Sauce Nantua
(Roulade of sole and watercress served with a Nantua seafood sauce)

Agneau de la Nouvelle Saison de Windsor au Basilic
(New season lamb herbed with Windsor basil)
Courgettes et Radis Sautées
(Sauteed courgettes and radishes)
Panaché d'Haricots Verts
(Mix of green beans)
Pommes Boulangère
(Oven-baked potatoes)
Salade
(Fresh green salad)

Charlotte à la Vanille et Cerises Griottes
(Vanilla Charlotte garnished with sour cherries)

Fruits de Dessert (Fruit selection)

Head chef, Mark Flanagan, replaces one of the copper cooking pots still in use today in the kitchens at Buckingham Palace. Some of them date back to the reign of King George IV. (PA Images)

ROYAL WEDDINGS

Royal marriages in the past were primarily diplomatic and dynastic unions that served to strengthen a family or families' hold on power and the Crown. The bride and groom often had no say over who they married, nor in how the wedding ceremony itself would pan out; weddings followed a strict protocol and other than changes in taste in terms of fashion and food, mostly followed a fairly set pattern.

All of that has changed these days, and members of the royal family have much more choice about whom they marry and how, although there are still guidelines and expectations governing both. Given the avid public and media interest and speculation that surrounds the events, participants are hard pressed to retain a degree of privacy. Despite this, royal weddings are without a doubt special occasions – a chance for regal pomp and pageantry to be expressed to its full – and prompt many thousands of well-wishers to line the streets to express their joy and support.

Elizabeth to Philip Mountbatten
20 November 1947, Westminster Abbey

The marriage between the future Queen and Lieutenant Philip Mountbatten was a wonderful public occasion, providing a desperately needed shot of colour and excitement to the austere post-war period. It was attended by 2,000 guests, and some 200 million people around the world listened to the ceremony on the radio. Elizabeth's father, King George VI, was so moved by the experience that he later wrote: 'I was so proud of you and thrilled at having you so close to me on our long walk in Westminster Abbey, but when I handed your hand to the Archbishop I felt that I had lost something very precious.'

After the ceremony, Elizabeth and Philip honeymooned at Earl Mountbatten's home in Hampshire and then at Birkhall on the Balmoral Estate. Afterwards, they temporarily lived in Buckingham Palace while they waited for their marital home, Clarence House, to be made ready.

Margaret to Antony Armstrong-Jones
6 May 1960, Westminster Abbey, London

The Queen's younger sister Margaret was a renowned socialite and something of a firebrand who liked to test the boundaries of monarchy. This she certainly did when she announced that she was going to marry Antony Armstrong-Jones, a photographer who moved in fashion, theatre and design circles – and not of noble blood. Nevertheless, Margaret got her way and was duly married to Armstrong-Jones, who was then titled 1st Earl of Snowden, in Westminster Abbey. This was the first royal wedding to be televised. The newlyweds made their home in an apartment in Kensington Palace and had two children before the turbulent marriage failed. In 1978 Margaret became the first senior royal to divorce since Henry VIII.

Anne to Mark Phillips
14 November 1973, Westminster Abbey, London

Princess Anne, aged 23, married fellow equestrian Captain Mark Phillips at Westminster Abbey in

Princess Elizabeth and the Duke of Edinburgh after their marriage ceremony, November 1947. (PA Images)

November 1973. As had happened at previous weddings, hundreds of thousands of well-wishers took to the streets to cheer on the couple and the ceremony was watched by an estimated 500 million television viewers worldwide. The marriage was to last 19 years, during which time the couple had two children, Peter and Zara. The couple announced their separation in 1989 and divorced in 1992.

Charles to Diana Spencer

29 July 1981, St Paul's Cathedral, London

It was billed the 'wedding of the century' by an enthusiastic press. So, when the Archbishop of Canterbury, Robert Runcie, spoke of fairy tales, the fanciful image caught the public mood. On the big day, Britons enjoyed a national holiday and thousands held street parties to mark the occasion and celebrate with the royals. Indeed, such was the importance of the occasion that the Poet Laureate, Sir John Betjeman, was moved to write in his celebratory poem that he fancied that even the blackbirds in city churchyards hailed the dawn of the wedding day.

Left: Captain Mark Phillips and Princess Anne leave Westminster Abbey after their wedding in 1973. (PA Images)

Below: Charles and Diana's wedding party in the throne room of Buckingham Palace. Back row, left to right: Edward Van Cutsem, Lord Nicholas Windsor, Sarah Jane Gaselee, Prince Edward, Prince Charles, Princess Diana, Prince Andrew and Lady Sarah Armstrong-Jones. Front row, left to right: Catherine Cameron, India Hicks and Clementine Hambro. (Getty)

Meanwhile, a 600,000-strong crowd took to the streets of London, hoping to catch a glimpse of the royal couple as they made their way to St Paul's Cathedral to exchange their vows. Around 750 million more television viewers worldwide watched as Lady Diana, dressed in an ivory silk taffeta and antique lace gown designed by Elizabeth and David Emanuel, made the three-and-a-half minute walk up the red-carpeted aisle. It was the most watched programme ever broadcast at the time, and went down in history as an iconic royal wedding.

Charles to Camilla Parker Bowles
9 April 2005, Windsor's Guildhall

Nearly nine years after the death of Diana, Prince Charles finally married his long-term love Camilla Parker Bowles. It was a small, private civil wedding at Windsor's Guildhall, witnessed by Prince William and Camilla's eldest son Tom Parker Bowles. Afterwards, the couple returned to Windsor Castle for a service of blessing at St George's Chapel, led by the Archbishop of Canterbury, Dr Rowan Williams. Around 800 family and friends attended, including the Queen and Prince Philip. The Queen hosted a reception in Windsor Castle's State Apartments, and according to guests gave a speech in which she wished the couple well.

William to Catherine Middleton
29 April 2011, Westminster Abbey, London

The wedding of Prince William to his university sweetheart and girlfriend of eight years Catherine Middleton was without a doubt one of the biggest events in royal history. About a million well-wishers lined the London streets, and some 34 million viewers tuned in to watch the ceremony in the UK, joined by a further 25 million in the USA. In total, it was estimated that more than 1 billion people watched the royal wedding coverage globally.

As Catherine walked up the aisle of Westminster Abbey on the arm of her father, Michael Middleton, the pomp and pageantry of centuries of royal tradition were on show, invoking a sense of national pride in the hearts of many. In honour of the occasion, a national holiday was declared and street parties were held all over the country, and indeed events were held in many parts of the Commonwealth.

The cost of the event is estimated at about £23.7 million, which was met by the Royal Family and the Middleton family, although security and transport were funded by the Treasury. In lieu of wedding presents from their guests, the couple requested that donations were made to selected charities.

Harry to Meghan Markle
19 May 2018, St George's Chapel, Windsor

The spectacular wedding between Prince Harry and American actress Meghan Markle on 19 May 2018 sent the USA into a media frenzy. Held in the ancient St George's Chapel at Windsor Castle, it was a traditional Church of England ceremony, with the Archbishop of Canterbury Justin Welby officiating at the wedding. But it also reflected the bride's background, with the inclusion of elements from African American culture. The Most Reverend Michael Curry, presiding bishop and primate of the Episcopal Church gave a memorable 14-minute address in which he spoken of the redemptive power of love and quoted American Civil Rights leader Dr Martin Luther King Jr.

One of the highlights was when The Kingdom Choir, a gospel group led by Karen Gibson sang 'Stand By Me'. The wedding was described as a 'landmark for African-Americans' and for black and dual heritage women, as well as for the royal family itself.

Opposite: Prince William and Catherine, Duchess of Cambridge make their way out of Westminster Abbey followed by maid of honour Philippa Middleton and Prince Harry, Prince Charles and Carole Middleton, Camilla and Michael Middleton after the wedding service. (Getty)

Prince Harry and Meghan, Duchess of Sussex, ride in an open-topped carriage through Windsor Castle after their wedding in St George's Chapel in 2018. (PA Images)

ROYAL BAPTISMS

Most royal babies are christened at royal palaces. Princes Charles and Prince William were both christened in Buckingham Palace's Music Room, while Prince Harry was christened in St George's Chapel, Windsor Castle. Princess Charlotte, however, was christened at the Church of St Mary Magdalene at Sandringham in Norfolk, arriving at the ceremony in a vintage 1950s silver-wheeled Millson pram.

In general, the christenings themselves are very traditional, following customs passed down through the generations. Many of the babies wear the royal christening robe, a replica of the original Honiton lace and satin robe made in 1841.

Although some members of the public are fascinated by royal christenings, they are usually private, family affairs; photographs and television footage of the guests and godparents arriving are generally released to the media only after the event.

The most recent royal baptism was the christening of Prince Harry and the Duchess of Sussex's son Archie Harrison Mountbatten-Windsor on 6 July 2019. The ceremony was held in the Private Chapel at Windsor Castle and was an intimate, private affair, attended by fewer than 25 immediate family members and close friends. Neither the Queen nor Prince Philip attended.

The couple shared some images taken on the day by photographer Chris Allerton, but declined to release the names of their son's godparents.

The christening robe

The new robe was created by the personal assistant and senior dresser to the Queen, Angela Kelly, after the original was deemed too fragile for further use. Despite its later exalted status, the original Victorian gown, which entered the record books after having been worn by more than 60 royal babies during its lifespan, had humble beginnings. The gown's creator was a young woman called Janet Sutherland, the daughter of a coal miner from Falkirk, who had been commissioned by Queen Victoria to make the gown for the christening of her eldest daughter, Victoria, Princess Royal, in 1841.

Mimicking the style of the wedding dress the Queen had worn for her marriage to Prince Albert the year before, the christening gown was made of Spitalfields silk with a Honiton lace overlay. In her diary, Queen Victoria described it as 'a white Honiton point lace robe and mantle over white satin' and wrote that her daughter had looked 'very dear' in it. Sutherland went on to receive the title of Embroiderer to the Queen, though she didn't hold this post for very long as she died at the age of 45.

In the 163 years that followed, the gown was worn by all royal babies, including Princess Elizabeth, Prince William and Prince Charles. After each ceremony it was hand-washed with spring water before being stored in a dark room, but by 2004 it had become too fragile for use and the new gown was commissioned.

The Lily Font

The gown was not the only part of the ceremony that Queen Victoria had a hand in. In 1841 she also commissioned the Lily Font, which has since been used at all royal christenings except that of Princess Eugenie, who in 1990 became the first royal baby to have a public baptism, at the parish church of St Mary Magdalene in Sandringham.

According to tradition, the water used is holy water from the River Jordan, where it is said Jesus was baptised by John the Baptist. Part of the Crown Jewels, the Lily Font is made of ornate silver gilt. It is decorated with lilies and ivy foliage around the rim, features three cherubs around the base, and the main bowl is a large lily bloom.

Queen Elizabeth, The Queen Mother, holding baby Prince William after his baptism at Buckingham Palace, the last occasion on which the antique christening robe was used.
(PA Images)

ROYAL FUNERALS

It's a strange fact, but preparations for the Queen's funeral began before those of her father, King George VI, who died in 1952. Since then, staff under leadership of the earl marshal, the Duke of Norfolk, meet occasionally to update the arrangements.

State Funerals

A state funeral is usually reserved for a monarch or an immediate member of the royal family. The last such funeral was held in 1952 for King George VI. In addition, very exceptionally, a state funeral may be held to honour a highly distinguished figure, as was the case upon the death of Sir Winston Churchill in 1965.

The ceremony itself follows very strict protocol and contains many traditional elements, as well as overtones of military tradition. First, the coffin, draped with the Royal Standard topped with the Imperial State Crown, is transported on a horse-drawn gun carriage to Westminster, accompanied by mourners, officials and military contingents. Here, it lies in state for, usually, three days, during which members of the public can file past and pay their respects. Throughout this time the coffin is guarded by four members of the Sovereign's Bodyguard and the Household Division.

After this, the coffin is carried by the late monarch's equerries from Westminster to Paddington, accompanied by employees, military contingents, Commonwealth representatives and other mourners. The family follows the procession, which ends at Paddington station.

Here, the coffin is loaded on to a train and, together with the mourners and officials, travels to Windsor, where the procession reforms and makes its way to St George's Chapel at Windsor Castle. Here, the funeral service takes place, following the Book of Common Prayer. Afterwards the coffin is placed in the family vault, and the Lord Chamberlain breaks his white stave of office – signifying the end of his period of service.

Philip, Duke of Edinburgh, Prince William, Earl Spencer, Prince Harry, and Charles, Prince of Wales walk behind Diana's casket during the funeral procession of the, Princess of Wales. (PA Images)

Ceremonial funerals

Other funerals, including those of senior members of the royal family and high-ranking public figures, may share many of the characteristics of a state funeral without being gazetted as such. These are called 'ceremonial funerals'. The funerals of Diana, Princess of Wales (1997), the Queen Mother (2002) and former Prime Minister Margaret Thatcher (2013), were in this category.

Did you know?

Each royal funeral has a code name. The Queen's is 'London Bridge' while that of her husband Prince Philip is 'Forth Bridge'. The late Queen Elizabeth's funeral was known as 'Tay Bridge', while George VI's was 'Hyde Park Corner'.

COMMON Q&AS

Q) WHY DIDN'T THE QUEEN'S ROYAL STANDARD FLAG FLY AT HALF MAST OUTSIDE BUCKINGHAM PALACE WHEN DIANA DIED?

A) *The Royal Standard is flown to indicate that a monarch is in residence. The reason why it was not lowered at the time of Diana's death was that the Queen was at Balmoral, which meant that the Royal Standard was not being flown at all at Buckingham Palace.*

Furthermore, the Royal Standard is never flown at half mast, even after the death of a monarch, because it is immediately replaced with the Royal Standard of their successor, the new monarch.

In response to the outcry, however, it was decided that the flagpole at Buckingham Palace should not be empty when the Queen was not in residence. Now the Union Flag (Jack) is flown when the Queen is not in residence, which means that that can be lowered to half mast when members of the family die or at other times of national mourning.

INDEX